THRESHOLDS TO PRAYER

Thresholds TO Prayer

— ⁓ —

KATHY COFFEY

ST. ANTHONY MESSENGER PRESS

Cincinnati, Ohio

Cover illustration by Jo Ellen McElwee
Cover design by Mary Alfieri and Karla Ann Sheppard
Electronic pagination and format design by Sandy L. Digman

ISBN 0-86716-295-3

Published by St. Anthony Messenger Press
Printed in the U.S.A.

CONTENTS

—— ❧ ——

For Mike, who mopped floors, drove children,
attended volleyball games and cleaned the
kitchen so this book could be written

ACKNOWLEDGMENTS

———————— ✣ ————————

The author thanks Art Winter, former editor of
Praying magazine, who suggested the columns
that form the basis of this book, and Dawn
Gibeau, current editor, for her permission
to reprint them.

INTRODUCTION

———— ॐ ————

Cartographers and geographers like their borders clear-cut; here (in blue) is France; there (the dusky rose) is Spain. So we are taught another border: To enter a church is to come into a different, sacred space. The language is formal; our behavior changes. We pause mid-sentence to become collected, quiet, reverent. Laughter is permissible only rarely and in certain spots—if the homilist tells a joke, for instance. Children taught that church is like a banquet or a party are puzzled; church behavior is more subdued than that at any party they've ever attended!

Contrary to this ingrained instinct, theologian Karl Rahner has helped us understand that our formal worship lifts up our grace-filled daily experience, already permeated by God's presence. It's not as if God visits us only in church. God is constantly revealed to us in the people, places and events we ordinarily encounter.

Distinct borders, then, between "church prayer" and what I'll call "everyday prayer" are misperceptions. Given the fact that God is always and everywhere seeking and creating us, and we are responding to that initiative, how can we draw distinctions? In this dynamic, no bold black lines proclaim, "Here ends prayer. Here begins life."

Perhaps they are not separate states but overlapping zones. It may seem hazy to those who like the clarity and order of graph paper. But it also seems logical that when we

1

consider holy mystery, we must abandon the security of our charts. Empty-handed, we approach the God who is beyond all our imaginings, all our categories, all our words.

God pervades all of our lives; were anything separate from God, the life-source, it would not exist. Thus, prayer and what we might label more "ordinary" experience spill into each other. The threshold experience works both ways.

Here is an example of how this process works. It is a traditional one; others in this book will show how prayer can spring from more unexpected sources. For now, let's say I begin the day by praying for my friend, recently diagnosed with cancer. I ask that she and her family come to peace with the hard path ahead. Boldly, I plead for complete healing. Most experts would identify this as a prayer of petition, pure and simple.

But as this prayer spills into my day, the borders start to vanish. The blue of France and the dusky rose of Spain blend into a pale violet watercolor. I start to see the opportunities presented to me in a new light. I realize that I am not immune from a similar diagnosis down the road; I know my time with doctors and hospitals will inevitably come. But, filled with sympathy for my friend, I understand I've had a reprieve. My current good health has bought me a little more time—time that, sadly, she will probably not have. How well will I use it? This hint of death and finitude could shadow the day; I could become depressed by the futility of our efforts. Will it all culminate in a doctor's stark words, a stranger's attempt at compassion? Before I go any further down that road, a voice which can only be God's self-revelation interrupts. Scripture and tradition tell us that any human life, no matter how brief, is a beautiful flowering. Created by God, we are uniquely gifted and upheld in life. The presence of death can paradoxically create a surge of life. To enter into that mystery is itself a little resurrection.

The acid test of prayer may be the question: What comes next? If it's only airy speculation, I may have wasted precious hours. But if it affects the texture and tempo of lived experience, then it is time well spent—time that will color all my moments with its depth and chorus of tones.

Two words become hinges on the door that opens this day. They aren't churchy words, but they are profoundly meaningful: *diagnosis* and *reprieve*—the shadow and the grace. Bearing them in mind, I will make decisions carefully. I will be at once more stingy and more generous. I'll skimp on time devoted to detail: the coupon-clipping and nit-picking that couldn't possibly rate a blip on the importance scale.

Yet the awareness that I will not have my family and friends forever (and they will not always have me) may prompt more generosity toward them. When will this son, who desperately wants me to take him skiing, be this young again? How soon will he take off independently, not caring whether I ski with him or not? How soon will this daughter be off to college, our times together compressed into holidays and vacations? Surely we should seize the rare chance for a leisurely breakfast together.

The perspective given by prayer turns the burden of obligations into the happier face of gifts, challenges and opportunities. Yes, I have a ton of work piled on my desk. But perhaps I should be grateful that my writing is in demand, that I have friends' letters to answer and the energy to give the tasks. Yes, my family can be greedy for attention. But how empty life would be without them! Sure, our house requires a lot of work. But how many people are homeless?

How much can spring from one still starting point! A wide variety of people and occasions can prompt prayer; prayer then shapes and influences our relationships and experiences. As it spreads across the day, giving it color, texture and meaning, prayer seems like the river without banks, the country without borders. To cross its threshold is to enter a world unlike ours, yet deeply connected with ours. Blessing of blessings, God freely crosses this threshold, too. The door opens both ways.

PART ONE

---- ॐ ----

A Cloud of Witnesses

They come into our lives like surprises, these mentors who are precisely the blessings God chooses to send. At first we may not suspect how much we need them, how our laughter will resonate, how deeply they will understand or how we will grow together. But we welcome them like gifts, perhaps hearing echoes of Flannery O'Connor's prayer:

> O, Raphael, angel of happy meetings,
> send us to those we are looking for
> send us those who are looking for us.

Rosie's Kitchen

Rosie was round as her pasta pot and plump as a ripe tomato. She would beam on my sons as they were digging into their third helping of spaghetti and lavishly smearing sauce across their faces. She begged my family to eat more, sabotaged our diets and pouted if we didn't scarf down seconds. It may not be fashionable to revere things like meatballs, but I still like to think of the ice cream she piled on the peach pie, the sweet gleam melting over the warm fruit.

Rosie has been gone for many years now, but I still think of her whenever I meet the image of God's hospitality. In Proverbs 9:4, God invites us "Come, eat of my bread, drink the wine I have mixed!" Because of Rosie's kitchen, I can appreciate a God who pours wine like a ruby cascade and lures us into abundant life. The God of feast and banquet appears frequently in the Old Testament (see Isaiah 25:6-7). Jesus often used the meal as a teaching moment. As Robert Karris writes: "The aroma of food issues forth from each and every chapter of Luke's gospel."[1]

When I become too focused on problems and too concerned about scarcity, I forget that grace abounds—as close as the kitchen table. If God is so intimately involved with the basic human activity of eating, so God must also be part of other ordinary actions. In a busy week, it is good to know that my avenues to God are no farther away than my daily routines. I needn't drive to church to find holy ground: I cross it constantly.

For instance, I hate to admit how much time I waste looking for lost objects. "I know I left the car keys on top of the TV!" I wail, frantically hunting under couches and coats. Even nuclear physicists must wonder about that mysterious black hole where socks and pens disappear. But faith can recognize another dimension in this seemingly futile hunt.

What a relief it is to know that God also spends time looking for the lost. The woman searching for the drachma is a biblical image of God. A contemporary image is provided by the mothers of the disappeared who call oppressive governments to accountability. In our own country, persistent parents track down their children to rescue them from the worst drug scenes. One mother, asked why she braved encounters with gun-toting heroin dealers to find her son, replied simply, "If I don't, who will?"

Compared to her brave commitment, my own quests pale, but they give us a taste of God's determination. If we have ever been desperate to find a child's book report before the car pool honks, we know the compelling nature of God's desire for us. And if we have experienced the thrill of unearthing the missing check, we know, too, how reassuring it is to be found. As the broom clinks against the lost coin, the woman rejoices. Such a small, daily victory can shape hopeful attitudes toward repentance and forgiveness.

Much has been written about the presence of God in the positive dimensions of parenthood. Like a good mother or father, God cajoles us to grow, enables us to serve, rewards our attempts and showers us with more opportunities. Last winter, my friend James taught his daughter Kate to ski. At first, she slid down the bunny slope braced between his legs. Then they climbed a little higher. Gradually she became more independent. By the end of the day Kate tackled steeper slopes alone, with confidence. In James's pride as he recounted Kate's progress, I caught a glimpse of our parent God: always leading us higher, cushioning our falls and applauding our efforts.

God can also be found in the downside of parenting, the bitter disappointments. A lovely older woman, faithful to the service of her church and family for many years, spoke with bewilderment about her children. "My son married an alcoholic. My daughter is pregnant and unmarried." The question must have plagued her: Where did I fail? What should I have done differently? The same ache resonates as God asks, "What more was there to do for my vineyard/ that I have not done in it?" (Isaiah 5:4). We are not alone in our anguish; God bears it, too.

The most mundane tasks do not escape the presence of God. Few people can avoid the mountain of laundry that accumulates at the end of the hall or overflows the hamper by Friday. Yet God enters even into that distasteful job. The psalmist prayed, "[W]ash me, and I shall be whiter than snow" (Psalm 51:7). He must have known how frequently we fail, how often we need the cleansing grace. And this insight penetrates this menial task with its maddening repetition. "The only way you can fail at prayer is to not show up," says Thomas Keating. Maybe prayer is like laundry.

Maybe all our cooking, losing, finding and washing are themselves a prayer. Now and then we recognize the face of God in these routine tasks. Elizabeth Johnson quotes a woman named Inez saying, "If they would ask me to draw God, I would draw my grandmother smiling."[2] If asked, I would draw Rosie, her face flushed, over a bubbling kettle. Something holy simmered in her kitchen. Something of God shone in her face.

Notes

[1] Robert Karris, *Luke: Artist and Theologian: Luke's Passion Account as Literature* (New York: Paulist Press, 1985), p. 47.

[2] Quoted in Elizabeth Johnson's *She Who Is: The Mystery of God in Feminist Theological Discourse* (New York: Crossroad Publishing Co., 1992), p. 146.

Praying With Mary Luke Tobin

Sister Mary Luke Tobin has an impressive list of accomplishments: one of three North American women invited to the Second Vatican Council; superior general of the Sisters of Loretto; president of the Leadership Conference of Women Religious; recipient of awards from *U.S. Catholic*, Call to Action, Women's Ordination Conference and numerous other organizations; founder of the Thomas Merton Center for Creative Exchange. In addition to these public achievements, she has changed my life by acting as a personal mentor.

Whenever I feel slightly paralyzed by the challenges confronting the Church in the nineties, I think of what she contended with in the Church of the sixties. The advent of women at Vatican II was historic; judging from the attitude of some cardinals, one would have thought the world was ending. It's somewhat startling, then, to see pictures of these women, many in full habits, as they filed into St. Peter's. In their sensible shoes and long veils, they looked about as threatening as kindly grandmothers. Yet Robert McAfee Brown referred to Luke and another auditor:

> When she and Sister Ann Richard invaded St. Peter's as almost the only women in a Council of over 2000 bishops (male), the authorities thought that they could cope with a 2000 to 2 ratio, only there was in their calculations this slight catch:
> That it turned out to be an even match.[1]

Luke was an extraordinary leader among them. While many religious of her era were docile and passive, she was articulate and assertive. While many women at that time were trained to defer to men, she confronted them fearlessly—at one point even tracking a bishop to his hotel room to win some acknowledgment! She laughs as she recalls some of her battles: "Women religious wanted some say in the decisions that would profoundly affect their lives. Seems fairly obvious, doesn't it? But we couldn't get it!"

In her book *Guests in Their Own House: The Women of Vatican II*, Carmel McEnroy tells an anecdote of Luke and Cardinal Antonucci. After having many disagreements throughout the Council, he told her good-bye: "I want you to know, Sister, that what I did...I did for the good of the Church."

She replied, "I too, your Eminence. What I have done...I believe I have done for the good of the church."[2] Two people can express their love for the Church in two different ways. As the contemporary Church becomes more polarized, I keep those words in mind. The common ground for all who remain, regardless of our particular bent, is our love for the Church.

Luke's past achievements and long record of service are remarkable on their own. But now, at ninety, she still finds the energy to maintain her daily swim, on-going ballet and continued commitments. This makes her a persuasive speaker on the subject of prayer: To someone with a track record like that, we pay attention.

And we are not disappointed by flimsy pieties. She quotes Thomas Merton, a close friend: "There is no contradiction between prayer and action when both are raised to the level of love." This is no pie-in-the-sky advice. Luke speaks of spending a half-hour every day to orient herself, to center on God's presence within, to say "yes" to God.

She then carries out that "yes" in action for justice: confronting governors, senators or company presidents about unjust treatment of migrant workers or environmental pollution. "Of course I don't like confrontation," she admits. "But I try to remember that within the person I confront is a marvelous capacity for the fullness of God."

Citing Karl Rahner, she praises the sublime gift: "God is continually giving God's self to us in a free, radical and absolutely profound and unmerited manner. It's a gift!" she muses. "I don't have to be good to merit this; I just have to be human."[3]

Coming to believe that insight more and more over the years has led to her feeling more relaxed about her human flaws. If she's touchy and cantankerous now and then, she expects it, and doubts that it's terribly important to God. What matters far more is "God's self-communication and presence moving into me. If I live another fifty years, I hope that will deepen so it will become a kind of constant atmosphere of my life."[4]

It's that ongoing optimism and humor that make Luke so attractive, still an internationally sought-after speaker. (At one Merton conference where she received a lengthy standing ovation, she quipped, "How about that, Tom?" When the microphone screeched an unintended response, she laughed as heartily as everyone else.) Her buoyant spirit is contagious. She instills her positive attitude in others, convincing them of Merton's belief that "You have all you need." When I was making some tentative beginnings as a poet, she stoutly proclaimed that I was the finest Catholic poet writing—with the single exception of her old friend Denise Levertov! When I sent her the first copies of my books, she was quick to respond with affirmation and congratulations.

With her formal religious training and background, one might expect Luke to be "churchy." Far from it. She puts into action the Vatican Council's emphasis on ecumenism, encouraging people of all traditions to join her quest. When Muslim people died in an attack on Palestine, she was one of the first to visit the local mosque with condolences and support. Her participation in international missions for peace has taken her throughout the world. Closer to home, she supports Church reform groups in Denver, despite long-winded, late-night meetings. On the picket lines, in jail and at board meetings, she continues to be a sign of hope.

In her life, those close to her can see her beliefs take flesh.

"Jesus wrote the chapter headings. We fill out the chapters, contexts and translations," she affirms, then goes out and does it.

Just considering her lifetime of work might leave the rest of us exhausted, but she is low-key and practical. It's nothing, she might say. Just one person's response to the marvelous reality of God's continual presence accompanying us throughout our days. We should all live so fully, so responsively, so prayerfully.

Notes

[1] Quoted in Carmel McEnroy, *Guests in Their Own House: The Women of Vatican II* (New York: Crossroad Publishing Co., 1996), p. 204.
[2] McEnroy, pp. 167-168.
[3] Kathy Coffey, "Prayer and Action, Action and Prayer: An Interview with Mary Luke Tobin," *Praying 35* (March/April 1990), p. 21.
[4] Coffey, p. 21.

On Retreat

There's only one way to eat institutional food: fork in with gusto and joke a lot. I have survived many a dismal convention meal because I could laugh with the people who shared it. But when a chunk of broccoli reared its ugly head in my vegetarian lasagna, my usual coping mechanism was out: I was making a silent retreat.

Last time I had arrived at the retreat center with four friends and two boxes of wine. You can guess our agenda. But this time I meant business and came alone, cold turkey. The week before and the week after the retreat were a chaotic maelstrom, but this week was to be an island of serenity. I had arranged myriad details on the home front just to be here and, by gum, I meant to get my hassle's worth.

I did. In God's gracious way I received more than I ever anticipated. I sank into long uninterrupted spaces as rare to a mom as surplus cash after the orthodontist's bills. I had time to smell iris spangled with dew and to watch a display of lightning that rivaled any Fourth of July fireworks. I luxuriated in reading late at night or early in the morning without the worry of disturbing anyone.

In our daily discussion, the retreat director gave suggestions for prayer that filled the silent spaces. He was wise enough to stop me when I'd gloss over a point of resistance, and sensitive enough to feed me fine books. I didn't always like the reflections he'd propose, but I would eventually discover they were tailor-made.

The prayer followed a logical progression, developed through long experience of the Ignatian exercises. I began by meditating on the many ways I have experienced God personally loving me. Inspired by that unassailable proof, I could then consider my own response. Often it had been inadequate. I had squandered God's gifts as wastefully as the parable's prodigal son or delinquent daughter. Tough as it was to admit these failures, they nevertheless gave me a grounding in grace. Describing this paradoxical dynamic, John Futrell writes: "If I really have the sense of God...I shall be reverent in the deepest way, because I shall be living humility, true poverty."[1]

Saddened yet empowered, I plunged ahead. My director recommended the story of Lazarus, with a personalized probe. "Where are you dead, paralyzed, bound? Ask Christ to touch that place." In the process of identifying this spiritual "closed fist," I found that my relationship with Christ had sadly eroded. In all my reading on the Trinity and work on social justice issues, I had forgotten the person at the center. When my director asked, "Have you talked to Jesus about this problem?" I was startled. I had imagined scenarios and conversations with everyone else I encountered, but had neglected the most crucial person.

Like the disciples on the road to Emmaus, I had lost "the one You who gave meaning to all their I's."[2] No wonder "they stood still, looking sad" (Luke 24:17). Like them, I had failed to recognize the source of all energy, the one whose belief in me nudges me into holiness.

I had wandered in an Emmaus fog, unable to see Christ's face. Yet his presence accompanied me, subtle yet certain as the scent of rain on the wind. He called to me as to Lazarus, and I came to trust his call. I began to appreciate how ironic it would be to refuse this invitation to fuller life. As Barry writes, "It may be God's ultimate heartbreak that he could not convince someone to trust him."[3]

So I admitted to Christ, "I don't want any block to come between us. If my failures would prevent my seeing your face, then I will bite my tongue, change my ways, do whatever I can to love better and act more responsibly." I suspect that when we take a mini-step toward God, God reaches for us with the long embrace of the parable's parent who stood waiting on the road, seeing the child far away.

During the retreat, I began to approach prayer with the enthusiasm Futrell describes: "I am going to meet God; I am going to have a personal encounter with my one great Love."[4]

In the weeks that followed the retreat, the prayer of Saint Ignatius echoed:

I choose You, Good Lord.
Count me among the victories that you have won in
bitter woundedness.
Never number me among those alien to You.

Some say a retreat is restful; I find it grueling work. But to
regain my center, it is worth the effort and the silent meals.
To focus again on Christ, I can endure broccoli sprouting in
my lasagna.

Notes

[1] John C. Futrell and Marian Cowan, *The Spiritual Exercises of Saint Ignatius of Loyola: A Handbook for Directors* (Hartford, Conn.: Jesuit Educational Center for Human Development, Inc., 1988).

[2] William A. Barry, *Paying Attention to God: Discernment in Prayer* (Notre Dame, Ind.: Ave Maria Press, 1990).

[3] Barry.

[4] Futrell.

Remembering the Martyrs

As the week ahead loomed stressfully, I whispered a litany to the martyrs of El Salvador. "Ignacio Ellacuria, Amando Lopez, Segundo Montes, Ignacio Martin-Baro, pray for us." As the week ended in a sense of peaceful fulfillment, I knew whom to thank. "Elba and Celina Ramos, Juan Ramon Moreno, Joaquin Lopez y Lopez, *gracias*." Through the challenges and gifts of every day, these Central American saints have been unfailing spiritual companions. So I will celebrate with special meaning November 16, the anniversary of their deaths.

What is the best way to honor the martyrs? The answer has several parts, but perhaps the first is by paying tribute to their ordinariness. Sanctity has its roots in the nitty-gritty, and they were no exception to this rule. I will muse on the mystery of Amando Lopez's African violets thriving in the haze of his Captain Black tobacco. I will recall how "Nacho," who had studied at the University of Chicago, could joke about the White Sox and play English songs on his guitar. I will smile fondly, knowing that Elba Ramos was just as worried about her beautiful teenage daughter as I am about mine. When I relax, I will remember Lopez y Lopez enjoying an "outrageously stupid" kung fu movie after a tough weekend of ministry in the countryside. As their former student, Jesuit Tim McMahon, said of their particular brand of holiness: "They were so ordinary. And if they could do it, so can I."

But there is more to the remembrance. The homey daily routine in San Salvador was also laced with grace. I revere the martyrs not so much for the way they died, but because they lived as a resurrected people. Elba Ramos owned very little. Yet, the day before she died, she washed her best dress to give to a woman displaced by bombing. She had stayed on campus that fateful night to make sure her husband got his supper. Aware of the increasing risk to his life, Segundo Montes said simply, "God's grace does not leave, so neither can we."

After thirteen years in the field, I know how much energy university teaching demands. So I can appreciate the Jesuits' commitment. No matter how busy they were with teaching, research or administration at the University of Central America, they devoted their weekends to the people of the poorest barrios and most forsaken patches of countryside. Five of them came from Spain, a more hierarchical society than ours, yet some gracious impulse prompted them to take their stand with people radically different from themselves.

In *Companions of Jesus*, his "small, unnecessary memoir," Jesuit Jon Sobrino summed up the message of his martyred brothers: "On this sinful and senseless earth, it is possible to live like human beings and like Christians."[1] When the evening news is depressing and the violence in our city escalates, I turn with hope to the Jesuit model. Though the civil war raged and the machine guns sprayed the streets of San Salvador, the Jesuit martyrs insisted on dialogue and negotiation. Ignacio Ellacuria's motto was "When the violence increases, we must think harder." When a crazed government wantonly tortured and murdered the poor, the Jesuits tenaciously repeated the gospel truth that these seemingly unimportant people were precious and unique.

As another Jesuit, Doug Marcouiller, said, "They loved something so much they put their lives on the line for it, and with great good humor." Doris Donnelly could have been describing them when she wrote, "Threatened and frightened people will protect all kinds of things: possessions, reputations, status, achievements. But redeemed women and men will count everything as folly, except service of the Lord. If that doesn't require a sense of humor, nothing I know does."[2]

So I shall celebrate the Jesuit martyrs with the laughter that defies death and the images that nurture life. I shall remember the symbols that spoke profoundly at the time of their deaths. I will remember the ways in which various Jesuit universities in this country commemorated the deaths. At Denver's Regis University, Kevin Burke crumbled wheat in his hands and scattered it on the chapel floor, saying softly, "Unless a grain of wheat falls to the ground and dies, it remains alone...." At Boston College, a drumroll followed the reading of each name and two thousand voices shouted, "Resurrexit!" The students at Santa Clara University made simple wooden crosses bearing each name and planted them in front of the mission church there.

Most poignantly, the husband of Elba and the father of Celina planted roses. Six red ones for the priests, two yellow ones for the women. Now they flourish on the ground that had once been wet with blood. That lush garden at the University of Central America is rich in resonance. Mary met the resurrected Christ in a garden. We meet him in the martyrs.

Notes

[1] Jon Sobrino, *Companions of Jesus* (Maryknoll, N.Y.: Orbis Books, 1990).
[2] Doris Donnelly, *Spiritual Fitness* (New York: HarperSanFrancisco, 1993), p. 120.

Grace During Dinner

I have been fortunate to have splendid mentors, but to have dinner with three of them simultaneously was a rare and wonderful occurrence. Since we all had the same publisher, he gathered us together and arranged a superb dinner. The conversation flowed as freely as the wine, and I suspect one reason we all had dessert was that we didn't want the evening to end. Picture them around the table: Miriam Therese Winter, Dolores Curran, Carmel McEnroy. When we look back on this era in Church history, I suspect we'll identify them as some of our most brilliant teachers.

When I first heard Miriam Therese at the Los Angeles Religious Education Conference, her ideas were so dramatic, I thought the top would burst off my head. As she presented her book, *The Gospel According to Mary*, I came to see clearly how long women had been excluded from Scripture, their stories edited out or altered, and how necessary it was to reclaim our rightful place there. In subsequent meetings and conversations, Miriam Therese encouraged me to write an imaginative view of women in Scripture. Her work thus led directly to my book *Hidden Women of the Gospels*.

At the time of our dinner, I was worried about her health. A vibrant woman usually filled with energy, she had undergone a mastectomy the previous month. Praying through her illness, I thanked God for the contribution she had made to women around the world. Her conversation at dinner was poignant as ever, but she seemed tired.

The next morning, Miriam Therese's convention keynote addressed six thousand people with joy and vivacity. I was familiar with many of her stories, but a hush fell over the audience when she began, "Last month I lost a breast to cancer...." I had thought she wanted to keep the matter private. Would she falter in this intimately personal revelation?

I should have known better. She explained how in recent years she had discovered the image of God as Shaddai, the breasted one, and how much it had come to mean to her. When she got the news of her cancer, she confided to a friend, with laughter and tears, "What a nasty turn of events. This is the pits!"

The same day, a package arrived in the mail. Friends had sent her a beautiful sculpture of Shaddai, the winged one. For Miriam Therese, gazing on it was like hearing God's voice saying, "You know I'm bigger than any language about me, any image for me. You've told lots of people—but you've forgotten yourself.... I'll be whatever you need!"

Dolores Curran has been a friend and mentor for years, a pioneer in religious education who first alerted us to the family as sacred space. She encouraged my writing, telling me I could do it *and* raise four children, and arranged for the first day of prayer I ever held. "Dolores, do you think anyone will come?" I asked tremulously. And no one laughed with more delight than Dolores when that retreat day filled and another for the overflow filled as well.

We were partners in crime when we launched a local newsletter, an alternative to the diocesan paper from which Dolores's column had been cut. We chortled together as we received national writing awards—we who'd been banned on the local scene! But for the first time that evening, I saw the sadness underlying Dolores's usual humor.

As we talked about her role in founding Call to Action, she remembered a time when she was forty-four, her children were young, and she had poured energy and time into an effort the bishops had requested. Then it had turned sour. After carefully developing and nuancing their recommendations, the group was publicly criticized, humiliated, castigated. All their arduous work met with scorn; many bishops turned their backs. "Ah," she sighed in retrospect. "We were such idealists!"

So am I, I realize, drawing on their gathered, rich experience to modify my naïveté. They have all had their confrontations with Church authority, yet still they remained joyous. Perhaps no one had endured a worse ordeal than Carmel McEnroy, fired from the faculty of St. Meinrad

Seminary because she had signed a *National Catholic Reporter* ad questioning the issue of women's ordination.

Despite her positive evaluations and tenure, she was fired with no due process and less than two weeks' notice. She comments on this dismissal: "The administrators' precipitous unilateral action against me evidenced, at best, their ignorance of the nuanced understanding of 'dissent' which clearly distinguishes honest differences from those that are hostile and obstinate."[1]

"Hostile and obstinate" are the last words that would come to mind in reference to this charming Irish sister, who regaled us with her stories over the merlot. When Dolores asked about emotional support from her religious community, she described the feisty, elderly Irish nuns who had been her firmest backers.

Carmel's book *Guests in Their Own House: The Women of Vatican II* underlines some of the discrimination against women taken for granted in the sixties. Only a few people thought it strange that the vast Vatican Council II should assemble without any women present. Cardinal Suenens was one who called attention to the disparity: "unless I am mistaken, women make up half of the human race."[2] In a sprightly style, Carmel recounts their stories, these women who made history by being the first ever to enter an ecumenical council.

In her own way, each woman at that restaurant table had been a prophet. Maybe they'll never be enshrined in stained glass or canonized. But I have a pretty good hunch when I'm in the presence of sanctity. That night I was. And I understood better why Jesus so often revealed himself in the context of a meal.

Notes

[1] McEnroy, p. 276.
[2] McEnroy, pp. 35-36.

Spiritual Direction

It's an ordinary-looking office, containing—as most offices do—a desk and computer, bookshelves, a couple of comfortable chairs. Yet when I have sense enough to come here, I see the place filled with grace. It is the office of my spiritual director.

For years I'd been reluctant to seek this kind of help, snickering silently at the oxymoron of the phrase "spiritual direction." Would making a regular appointment exaggerate the puny nature of my spiritual life? Was it simply another exercise in self-importance?

I wasn't facing any major crises; I was simply plugging along. I'd always thought spiritual direction was for the saints who worked with AIDS patients, or the newly bereaved, people wrestling with moral quandaries, or those confronting major life decisions. What would I discuss with a spiritual director—the relative merits of PBJ vs. turkey sandwiches in the brown-bag lunches I packed daily? "Well, there's the mayonnaise factor to consider..." I could solemnly intone.

But I'm beginning to see "things churchy" in terms of a support group. Those of us who come to church, or spiritual direction, aren't there because we're perfect. Like those who flock to Weight Watchers or Gamblers Anonymous, we're there because we know we need help. We may seem to be gliding smoothly along on the surface, but deep down we're like little kids lost in a vast discount store. Years of conditioning and social mores are all that stand between us and a frightened yelp, "Ma!"

What a relief to discover that the spiritual director's office is a safe place to yelp. There I can divulge that, despite apparent success, I still have enormous self-doubt, that I often squander the precious gifts I've been given, that despite continuous assurances of God's presence, I'm sometimes engulfed by depression. It's even more reassuring to know that the resident guru doesn't have all the answers, but is simply another fallible human being struggling with the same questions.

I don't want to make it sound like an exchange of ignorances. The staff at our local retreat house are holy men and women who have taken time to think long and hard about the issues that concern us all. They carve out a large part of each day for prayer, but that doesn't mean they are detached from reality: They, too, struggle with the bills and worry about that funny knocking noise in the car.

This contact with reality is exactly what makes them so helpful. It's difficult to take inspiration from a saint when I'm stuck in traffic or overwhelmed at work or fielding too many questions from the kids. But if I can think of another human being who, like myself, can and would make the right decision, I feel I can, too. I know that I am not alone in my struggles, that my failings are simply that— well-intentioned human weaknesses.

Spiritual direction isn't grains of advice dispensed from someone wiser or more prayerful than me. It's a chat between hikers on the same trail, a word between runners in the same race. We're all tired and aching, but in each other we find the encouragement to keep moving ahead.

Cyrus Resurfaces

It just happened again. Late for school, my daughter and I were struggling down the street with her backpack. (It looked as though she'd crammed the refrigerator and microwave in there. And maybe an axe, too.) The thought of walking to school together had seemed quaint—mother and daughter chatting chummily beneath the arch of autumn trees—until the reality hit. Then the pressure of time and the weight on our shoulders made the cozy morning plan seem like a nightmare.

Until a Jeep pulled up beside us. Other friends had sailed past on their way to school, waving merrily. (Probably inside the car, the moms had muttered darkly to their children that they should walk and be healthy like we were.) This was the first offer of a ride, and by that time it was welcome.

The funny part was the woman who offered the ride. We weren't exactly enemies, but I can't say I'd ever sought her company. Flung together in social situations, we'd managed to skirt the disagreements that hovered just below the surface and exchange momentary pleasantries. Somehow I sensed that if we ever really got into truthful discussion, it could quickly turn to raging argument.

Yet here she was, door flung wide, with the offer to retrace her path to school, where she'd just dropped off her own children. "C'mon—then you won't be late!" she promised Katie. As I waved them off, I had to chuckle. Cyrus had surfaced again.

Whenever help comes from an unexpected direction, I think of Cyrus. This king of Persia (559-529 B.C.) overthrew the Babylonian empire, delivered the captive Jews and allowed them to rebuild Jerusalem and the temple. While they had long looked for a savior and prayed for their deliverance, the way they were freed must have been something of a surprise. Isaiah names Cyrus the "anointed one" (45:1), a title reserved for the king, and imagines God grasping him by the hand. The prophet has God say to Cyrus, "I call you by your name,...though you do not know me" (45:4).

That story and my own surprises have made me wonder how often we act unwittingly as God's agents. If I have been saved by those I least suspected, then isn't the inverse true? A friend who gives retreats laughs about inadvertently saying the worst, most insulting things to people who then come up and tell her how much they appreciated her words. A priest recently admitted that he'd had time to prepare only half a homily, but it turned out to be one of the best he ever gave.

We all have our favorite examples—the day that looked disastrous but turned out OK; the person we initially disliked who grew into a fine friend; the job we tackled with gritted teeth that became rather pleasurable in the doing. With excruciating irony, I once told my son's friend to call back in three hours and *not* to disturb his sleep again. If I had engraved Cyrus' story more deeply—in the palms of my hands as they held the phone, for instance—I would have known. Two minutes after hanging up huffily on this young intruder—who had the gall to call at 8 A.M. on a holiday morning—I marched self-righteously to the car. Which wouldn't start. It's anyone's guess what young mechanic we had to summon (humbly) at that early holiday hour to get it going. Crow fricasseed, crow fried, crow en brochette, crow stew: I have all the recipes for anyone who needs tasty ways to eat it. How therapeutic to discover that I was in good company. Think of the traveler in the parable, lying bleeding beside the road. What a relief to see help approaching, then to realize, through a pain-filled haze, that help wore the clothing of the hated Samaritan. Nathan Mitchell comments, "How do you know the Samaritan won't kill you? You don't. You first have to trust, to take the risk of letting him pull you from the ditch. Only then can the stranger be recognized as a savior."[1]

We shouldn't be surprised that our Savior can take on different disguises. Recently, I seethed about the time I'd lose from a busy week to attend an overnight retreat (manadatory for work) in the mountains. As it turned out, we stayed in a beautiful setting where clouds of pussy willows lined a shining stream. In walks beside that stream, I was able to articulate issues that had simmered annoyingly beneath the surface. Of course, the woman I walked with, who listened sympathetically and helped draw me out, was another Cyrus in disguise.

Some of this woman's mannerisms had turned me off; I'd dismissed her because at times I thought she was coarse and outspoken. Yet—the saving grace again—she was the perfect companion for that interlude. During the week that followed, I'd return mentally to that mountain stream, picture the pussy willows and remember the message that had come there, "We have everything we need"—if we're not too dense to recognize it!

Notes

[1] Nathan Mitchell, *Eucharist as Sacrament of Initiation* (Chicago: Liturgy Training Publications, 1994), p. 27.

Praying With Spirit

It never fails to energize me. In her book, *She Who Is*, Elizabeth Johnson begins simply enough: "Let us speak of the Spirit's actions...." Then she's off on a splendid quest, an exploration so overflowing with activity that it might leave the raiders of the lost ark breathless.

When I taught creative writing, I'd warn my students, "Adjectives are the potbelly of the sentence. Verbs are your strong suit; they carry your power." Apparently the Spirit knows that strategy, too, for Johnson's language about God is all verbs, sinuous and tensile. Among some of the Spirit's activities, she lists "endure, delight, challenge, create, indwell, sustain, resist, recreate, guide, liberate, complete, play, suffer, sympathize, renew, participate, energize, empower, vivify, knit together, transform, heal, strengthen, comfort, invigorate, refresh, and uphold the world in pervading and unquenchable love."[1]

We may want to draw a deep breath before continuing, but the Spirit doesn't pause. Throughout the Scriptures, we find analogies between the activity of the Spirit and that of human beings. Like a midwife, she works with those in pain to birth a new creation (Psalm 22:9-10). In the midst of agony, Spirit-Sophia teaches people justice and courage (Wisdom 8:7). Wherever she inspires human beings, she moves them to bold confrontation with the powers and principalities that crush and oppress. Like a defense attorney, she bears witness to Christ (John 15:26-27). Like a baker, she kneads the leaven of kindness and peace "into the thick dough of the world until the whole loaf rises" (Matthew 13:33).[2] Through the mediation of human beings she washes what is unclean (Isaiah 4:4), heals what is hurt, warms what is frozen and straightens what is crooked.

I have often sung "Veni Sancti Spiritus" and love the hymn in all its varieties. But I never dreamed what a whirlwind of activity I was innocently inviting! It is dangerous risk-taking when we ask to mirror this Spirit in our actions.

Johnson's approach makes that daunting task seem

possible. Skillfully she researches the many feminine metaphors for God in Scripture, so that women who may not relate to images of warfare and fortresses can find images closer to their milieu.

The Spirit's activity comes near to home. We are not made to feel guilty if our area of effort is not the Third World. In any walk of life, we can bring the Spirit, and we can learn from oppressed peoples how to do so. Leonardo Boff, author of many books on liberation theology, writes, "the Spirit is that little flicker of fire burning at the bottom of the woodpile. More rubbish is piled on, rain puts out the flame, wind blows the smoke away. But underneath everything a brand still burns on, unquenchable.... The Spirit sustains the feeble breath of life in the empire of death."[3]

How often we battle in the kingdom of death! How often we struggle to maintain relationships that face the equivalents of rain, wind and rubbish threatening to quench the flame! When we intervene on behalf of our children, when we care for the sick, when we protest uninspiring liturgies and unfair Church policies, when we strike for justice, when we make efforts to live healthy and vigorous lives, when we try to bring a creative dimension into our work, we can be allied with the Spirit and strengthened by it.

Even as we struggle with change, the Spirit is with us, "to shake up assured certainties and introduce the grace of a new question."[4] The Spirit's presence constantly reassures: In the opening scene of the Bible, the Spirit hovers over the waters. At the end of the Bible, in the Book of Revelation, the Spirit promises, "See, I am making all things new" (Revelation 21:5).

Perhaps most touching is a gesture so tender it reminds us of a mother and child or two lovers together. The Spirit "will wipe away every tear from their eyes" (Revelation 7:17). As I do that little service for a sobbing child, I will remember: I am made in God's image. I act in imitation of God's Spirit. Then action becomes prayer. And prayer to the Spirit suffuses our days with dynamism and love.

Notes

[1] Elizabeth Johnson, *She Who Is: The Mystery of God in Feminist Theological Discourse* (New York: Crossroad Publishing Co., 1993), pp. 133-134.
[2] Johnson, p. 137.
[3] Quoted in Johnson, p. 137.
[4] Johnson, p. 138.

PART TWO

—————— ॐ ——————

A Chorus of Voices

We who live within the close circle of Christ's Mystical Body know that we do not stand alone. Nor do we pray alone. Crossing the threshold to prayer, we never leave behind the people who mean the most to us. Instead, we lift them up, praising and thanking God for them, asking God's blessing upon them.

Prayer also becomes a connection to those we do not know. As we intervene for people all over the world, we become mysteriously linked with them. So, when we enter the sacred space of prayer, a crowded, jostling, colorful procession accompanies us. Perhaps this is what Scripture means by sharing "in the inheritance of the saints in the light" (1 Colossians 1:12).

A Homily on the Mystical Body

True confession time: When homilies get dull, I find inspiration in the folks surrounding me. The reading about the body of Christ (1 Corinthians 12:12-27) is enfleshed all around the church.

She and he lean slightly toward each other, two white heads bent close, probably from long habit. Together they would not weigh more than 225 pounds. It is not hard to imagine them slipping into a single bed. But they are hardly the stereotypical apple-cheeked old woman and old man. As they turn to us at the kiss of peace, he seems genuinely delighted to greet my children; her eyes are filled with humor. When they leave Mass early, I speculate whether they're off to some pious project or, more likely, the tennis court.

Gradually, I remember their story. Before their hair turned white, their twenty-year-old son drowned. Mentally, I try to steel myself against that tragic loss of a child, ultimately giving up: It is too painful to imagine. At the time, a dazed parish community had surrounded them with affection, gauzy bandages held in hope against a bleeding wound. I wonder now (the homily droning on) how they have handled the impossible. Many marriages do not survive the loss of a child; how have they beaten the odds?

"God has so arranged the body,...that the members may have the same care for one another. If one member suffers, all suffer together with it" (1 Corinthians 12:24-26).

They had probably been the compassionate Christ for each other. They cried in each other's arms. She rubbed his back. He soothed her tears. She still leaned close to catch his whispers. He held her hand throughout the homily. Yet their affection was not sentimental. It was as though a tough, invisible bond warmed the air between them. In the right light, it would sparkle.

"As it is there are many members, yet one body" (1 Corinthians 12:20). If ever two people were united, the pulsing proof sat in the pew before me. Paul's text was written there, an indisputable argument stripped clean of verbiage, that love could outlive death.

"God is turned toward us; we image God when we are inclined toward another." When I heard this idea on a retreat, the director nodded toward the engaged couple who constantly leaned toward each other. But here I recognized the same posture, after many years, enduring many blessings and blows. I thought with gratitude of the people with whom I share such a bond: brushing shoulders, joking together, touching in this mysterious web. The mystical body is fragile, yet the strongest thing I know.

The homily rambles toward an end, and the choir starts the haunting hymn, "Now We Remain": "We hold the death of the Lord deep in our hearts...." Deep in their hearts, this couple had held the death of their son. Words strain to capture the mystery: Somehow, they had also cherished the broken body of Christ.

Today I also observe this liturgy of the word with children. There, the catechist Julie contends with another impossible situation: a session that begins with thirteen children of different ages and gradually swells to nineteen. Developmental stages are all over the map. The little boys poke each other. The girls look primly bored.

No matter. She has prepared dough, and they will bake pretzels in a shape symbolizing arms folded for prayer. As they roll their "snakes" and brush them with egg white, she converses simply with the children about prayer: "What makes you scared?" Spiders, it seems—and mean brothers. "Do you ever pray when you're scared?" The conversation meanders over the yeasty smell of rising dough: never didactic, gently inviting. Paul could easily be woven in: "the members of the body that seem to be weaker are indispensable..." (1 Corinthians 12:22).

Julie probably doesn't know canon law. I'd guess she is hazy on transubstantiation. But she is living proof that all the doctrines matter less than the slow, patient shaping of one individual at a time.

She ignores the chaos to edge close to each child. Perhaps it's only a few minutes of one-on-one time, but it means everything: to Amber, enduring her parents' divorce; to Cory, who seems unhealthily pale; to Lupe, who would never come to church if it weren't for Julie.

As the pretzels emerge warm and fragrant from the oven, I think how much is wrapped in those puffy shapes. They had risen like prayer, buoyed with the children's longings.

I relish irony. Passing the priest at the door, I murmur ambiguously, "Fine homily." All without a word.

A Small Circle of Friends

I am often uptight about praying in public, but every now and then it goes well. This was one of those times.

My friend Trish was facing critical spinal cord surgery. If she didn't have the surgery, she'd face paralysis. Even with the surgery, the chance of paralysis was fifteen percent. When she told me the prospects, it felt devastating, like a lose-lose situation. But with characteristic feistiness, she declared, "I've decided to be bold. I'm praying for total healing." If she could be that faith-filled, how could I be any less confident?

I suppose I turned to prayer out of desperation, not knowing what else I could do for my friend. Fortunately, a small group of us were gathering for a meeting, and having known each other for many years, all wanted to join in prayer for Trish.

As four men and four women spoke their thanks for Trish and their desire for her healing, it was as if we gathered our strength around her. As she was anointed with holy oil, we encircled her and touched her: Some touched her shoulders, one held her hand, one knelt and touched her leg.

Fortunately this group was familiar with the symbol of oil, how it had flowed over the foreheads of priests, prophets and kings. Trish's anointing stood in a long tradition: so Saul had anointed David, so Mary had anointed Christ. Just as athletes oil muscles before a competition, so the lovely fragrance would be balm for her skin, healing for her heart, strengthening for her spirit. At one time, Christians believed that if they were well oiled, the devil couldn't get a grip on them!

As Trish wept quietly, I remembered Joyce Rupp's story of a group of friends who'd gathered in a similar setting. To the friend who was preparing for surgery, they had given a stone which they had passed around their circle. All had prayed into that stone their heartfelt desire for her health, the strength they could share. The stone was then taped to the hospital gurney, and stayed throughout the surgery. It was a potent symbol that we do not go alone into the world's dark places; we carry each other along to offset the terror and pain ahead.

Our little ceremony was similar. Although there were a priest, a woman religious and two inactive priests in the group, no one was formally vested. Most of us wore blue jeans and sweatshirts. We gathered in a small living room, not a chapel or cathedral. No choir sang; no organ played. We had no script but our heartfelt wishes.

Without any of the usual accoutrements of public prayer, we nonetheless created a holy space and a deeply moving time. I suppose it's what people mean by the sacrament of the ordinary.

I hope Trish remembers it in the weeks ahead, as she signs forms in triplicate, undergoes testing and billing and poking and prodding. When she was a child, a surgeon had told her parents, "The spine is God's country." We will not suffer the needles or confront the paralysis, but for a few moments we entered that country with Trish. We will not be wheeled down the long white corridor to the operating room, but as much as grace and friendship allow, we will walk beside her there.

Henri Nouwen believes that when people put God first, God sends them the fine companions they need.[1] If I were in Trish's shoes, I would not confront crisis so bravely but would cling tightly to the anchor of my companions. Like her, I would be immensely grateful for the feel of oil on my skin, the touch of my friends, the sound of their voices praying for me. With such support, we can journey into the valley of suffering. Perhaps it's the only way we can go.

Notes

[1] Henri J. Nouwen, *Can You Drink the Cup?* (Notre Dame, Ind.: Ave Maria Press, 1996), p. 98.

Penetrating the Labyrinth

First, an admission: I've never been comfortable with bodily prayer. Intense intellectual training and a career in academia left me with a huge skull. I usually drag the body along like a clunking chariot. Naturally I'm skeptical of any attempt to draw the two together in prayer. The hootenanny link-arm style is too folksy for me. A Gothic nave and a silent pew are more conducive to contemplation.

Then I met the labyrinth. In common usage, the term represents chaos. Remember Francis Thompson, "I fled him down the labyrinthian ways of my own mind"? When we're embroiled in a confusing situation, we call it a labyrinth and focus on a one-way ticket: out.

But thanks to the Grace Cathedral Center for Spiritual Wholeness, the labyrinth has recovered its ancient meaning as a prompt for prayer. Modern people reclaiming this tradition are discovering in the labyrinth's archetypal paths the sacred nature of their daily steps.

While labyrinths are found in all the world's religious traditions, this contemporary replica is modeled after the one laid in the stone floor of Chartres Cathedral around 1220. Its eleven concentric circles extend forty-two feet in diameter. Those unable to visit either Chartres or the San Francisco cathedral can still experience a traveling labyrinth laid out on canvas.

When I had this opportunity, I entered a mysterious time warp and became a medieval pilgrim. After the crusades made travel to Jerusalem too dangerous and expensive for most people, the Vatican named seven European cathedrals as final destinations, domestic "Jerusalems." Entering the cathedral's labyrinth marked the end of a difficult journey, as well as the entry into an image of the Celestial City. For pilgrims who had spent two or three weeks on muddy fields and unpaved roads, the cathedral imaged heaven. The sun shining through stained glass created a dancing jewel; it did not require a great leap of the imagination to feel they had finally arrived.

The center of the labyrinth contains a six-petaled rose or lily. In the mystic tradition, the rose is a symbol for the Spirit; the lily for Mary. The center may also symbolize unity with the Holy One. It is a place of profound meditation.

But let's start at the beginning. As I stepped out in stocking feet onto the white canvas of the labyrinth, I must admit that my first impression was annoyance with the other people who shared the path. The way in is also the way out; meetings with others must be silently negotiated. As in much of life, the simple courtesies get us through. We work it out by stepping aside, pausing. I notice that some people are crying; other faces are ravaged by grief or fear. Some people limp, yet there is a trance-like beauty in reverent steps matched to the distant music of Gregorian chant. I start appreciating these strangers who share my pilgrimage: Did I just pass Chaucer's Wife of Bath?

Like all things human, the experience is punctuated with irreverence. With eyes on the floor, I meet people mostly through their socks and I can't help smiling at holey or mismatched ones or flashy argyles.

The labyrinth's three phases parallel the threefold mystical path. The way in is the path of purgation: letting go of the mental clutter that blocks prayer; stilling, emptying, releasing. The center represents illumination: a special, unique grace waits there to be received. The way out is the path of union: We leave renewed with the power to act, bringing our gifts to the service of the world.

Saint Augustine once said, "It is solved by walking." Perhaps he knew of labyrinth prayer, where the mind is quieted by the body's rhythmic motion. As I find my pace there, I become aligned with my best self. I let go of worries about getting lost, realizing that in the spiritual life, there is only one path. The nonverbal, experiential approach frees me to go within the immanent God.

The focus is not on the result but on the journey. Like my medieval ancestors, I discover that what matters isn't the rutted roads or the moldy bread but the Way. On my way out, I think of articles to write and classes to teach, but

I do not see them as burdens. I walk toward them with energy and anticipation, recognizing welcome outlets for my creativity. In the center of the labyrinth, I had stood in the presence of the Holy One. That presence accompanies me now as I go forth.

Eucharistic Duet

The duets in *West Side Story, Phantom of the Opera* or any musical blend male and female voices in a skillful weaving of tones. The two voices overlap, soar in waves above each other, crescendo together and meet in harmony.

The duet is not only the province of the professional singer. I recently attended a buoyant, uplifting Mass with a male friend. At first the music was unfamiliar, much of it in other languages. Yet as we shared the songbook, we ventured into this unknown territory with increasing confidence. He has a strong baritone voice; mine gained assurance as our voices joined with thousands of others. Chanting a Taize hymn over and over, we entered into its meaning, but more importantly into its spirit: *"Nade te turbe"* his voice assured me. *"Solo Dios basta,"* mine answered. We can talk all we want about trust in God, but it helps to hear the message in a human voice.

The duet is a good metaphor to keep in mind when we talk about the Eucharist. Just as the two voices meld, each distinct yet each giving depth to the other, so in this sacrament our lives mingle with Christ's.

His last supper discourse, positioned on the cusp of death, could be seen as a farewell aria. In it, a man who had been humble all his life speaks suddenly of glory. The concern he pours into his words is for his friends. As his life draws to a close, he wants it to count; like any human being, he wants to have made a difference. Unpromising as they may appear, those gathered around him at the table are his last, best hope for passing on his message. Jesus says to the Father, "As you have sent me into the world, so I have sent them into the world" (John 17:18).

As the heirs to those first disciples, our lives, too, are colored with Christ's meaning because they are mingled with his life. This is most clear during the liturgy when water dissolves in wine: a perfect symbol of two elements blending. We may think ourselves common as water; most of us claim few distinctions or awards. Yet we long for some majesty, some meaning. Our lives, when joined to Jesus', are no longer little. Jesus' whole purpose in becoming human was to expose the grandeur in your life, my life, every human life. It gleams there like some golden vein in a blue-black granite lode.

Because it's a difficult concept to grasp, the symbol speaks more profoundly than words. Within the crystal goblet, the wine catches glimmers of light. It stirs with mystery and opens secret windows. Those who drink it respond in their unique ways to Jesus' plea, "whenever you do this, remember me." Furthermore, we do not drink alone. We join with all those around the world, past, present and future, in the mind-boggling Communion of Saints.

We also unite with those who are physically present with us. As our faith community comes forward for Eucharist, we cannot imagine the specific places where we will bring the Good News in the week ahead. We do not know exactly how we will be bread and cup for a hungry world. But we draw on a deep assurance that we're all in this together. Mysteriously, all our efforts will join together, and this sacrament will spread far beyond the walls of our church.

Lifting the chalice, we hold reflectively our whole lives: unique and vibrant, full of cherished memories, nurturing relationships, unresolved dilemmas, unguessed potential, bounteous gifts. Then we drink—a full, deep, refreshing drink—in symbolic acceptance of all we are. In the wine, the spirit of Jesus pours through us, as if in answer to his petition, "that they may have my joy made complete in themselves" (John 17:13).

The poet Mary Oliver challenges us with the question: "Tell me. What is it you plan to do with your one wild and precious life?"[1] Having no dress rehearsals and only one life, we join it to Christ's. We come to Communion. Then the duet begins.

Notes

1 Mary Oliver, "The Summer Day," *New and Selected Poems* (Boston: Beacon Press, 1992), p. 94.

Symbolic Value

Being a poet attunes one to the value of the symbol. Being a Catholic poet adds a double dose: I am often aware of a second, spiritual level of meaning in almost every experience. (One of my creative writing students laughed about this perspective as she reminded herself, "It's only a door handle. Quit reading meaning into it!")

That introduction may explain why the symbolic value of a recent experience resonated clearly in retrospect. I had given a day of prayer at my favorite retreat house in the foothills. We had spent the day looking at Jesus' treatment of women and discovering how startling it was for his time. Given his cultural milieu, the way he touched women, conversed with them, learned from them and befriended them broke taboos with wild abandon. In the day's conversations, many women expressed a new appreciation for Jesus and a higher estimation of themselves.

All was going well, but I was concerned about the Eucharist we'd planned to conclude the day. The director of the retreat house was sympathetic to women's issues and had already asked me to give the scriptural commentary. But how could I sit passively through the rest of the service after taking a leadership role all day? I knew that Mass was a time for prayer, not a political agenda. But weren't there times when we had to speak up, subtle ways we could resist inequalities?

I spoke to Rich, the director, at lunch. "Look, we can't talk about Jesus' treating women as equals all day, then end at the door of the chapel. How can we model equality at the Eucharist without getting you into trouble?"

Even among Jesuits known for their brilliance, Rich has an extraordinary configuration of talents. He is wise and quiet; his passion for justice comes as something of a surprise, clothed in Louisiana courtesy. When the Belizean government needed someone to represent their country in negotiations for educational funding, they sent Rich to London. When the Mexican government needed expert ad-

vice on some recently uncovered documents, they sent for
Rich. When U.S. Jesuits wanted their best representation at
the congressional committee examining the murders of
Jesuits in El Salvador, they sent Rich. When a birth mother
and an adoptive couple wanted a blessing for their baby before the adoption was finalized, they asked Rich. Diverse
peoples recognized beneath his reserved demeanor tough
skills and gentle compassion.

He did not disappoint me either. Without a long discussion, he invited a religious sister and me to stand with
him from the Offertory and Consecration through Communion. As he held up the bread, we held up the chalices.
When he distributed the hosts, we offered the wine. I hope
someday it will all seem rather mild, but in many dioceses
in the nineties, two women flanking a priest at the altar
would not be welcomed with warm applause.

We acted as if we did it every day, as if it were natural
for men and women to stand together at the altar as they
did in every other arena of life. I felt as if I belonged there,
as if a long-delayed gift had finally arrived or a daughter
had returned home from a journey. Our stance seemed to
say, "It's all we can do for now. But the symbol represents
our hope for the future: a reconstituted Church, a disciple-
ship of equals." I wish my daughters had been there.

After most of the people had left, Rich and I moved
chairs in the conference room and collected coffee cups like
a pair of janitors. It was quiet and comfortable, like friends
cleaning up after a party, talking casually about how it had
gone. The solidarity we'd expressed at the altar rang true
because it carried over into the nittiest-grittiest areas of life.

For some time, I had been puzzled by the phrase "dis-
cipleship of equals." Elizabeth Schussler-Fiorenza had
coined the expression to explain what Jesus had in mind
when he called the first women and men to follow him. But
I'd seen so little equality in reality, I had no experience in
which to moor the high-sounding words.

"Let the new information replace the old" has always
been one of my favorite computer prompts. To days that

seem mired in sameness it introduces the possibility, indeed the reality, of change. Potential beckons like a distant shore; just around the next bend might be a lovely vista.

Holding the goblet of wine aloft that day, in the late afternoon sun of the wood-paneled chapel, encircled by a community of believers, I had that glimpse of potential. "When you do this, remember me," Jesus had said over just such a cup. Maybe "you" included all of us, regardless of gender. Maybe we were finally trying to comply.

Viva la Diversidad

It stands to reason that God who created a million kinds of animals, over 800,000 species of insects, and more than 600 varieties of eucalyptus trees alone would also create an equally stunning variety of ways to pray. In describing this infinite variety, formal liturgy may come to mind, but I want to explore here alternate forms of prayer, which correspond to our common experiences.

Just as women and men of the monastic tradition organized their days according to the hours of the Divine Office, so lay folk may discover its rhythms in their lives. Instead of following canonical texts, we find our prayer woven into the events at hand in our daily life.

Thomas Merton understood such correlations between his Trappist prayer tradition and ordinary life. He describes it this way:

> ...the psalms of the rain,
> of the odors and crackling of the fire
> the psalms of the stars and the clouds and the winds
> in the trees—all equally eloquent...
> the psalms of one's coughings and sneezings and coffee
> drinkings.[1]

In the course of a day, other prayer forms emerge. A Native American woman faces east at dawn. Admiring the apricot sky, she places herself in God's design, with the pines, hawks and grass. Some people punctuate the day with "arrow prayers"—straight shots to the heart of God. They may come as the thermometer in a child's mouth tops 104 degrees or the gas gauge nears empty. Others repeat the "Jesus Prayer" until it becomes as unconscious as inhaling. For them, the words "Jesus Christ, Son of God, have mercy on me, a sinner" correspond to the rhythm of every step, match their breathing and bring them to a deep place beyond thought.

Bodily prayer has a similar effect. Almost every culture has its sacred dances, and I once participated in the Indian form. Initial anxiety and self-consciousness soon gave way to a sense that my whole body was worshiping. Repeatedly I reverenced my partner with a deep bow and sang the ancient words, "Om, Shanti." As our gestures became increasingly graceful, we danced that space sacred and bent the lines between beauty and prayer. Perhaps there is no real distinction.

In the Benedictine tradition, the tools of our trades are treated with profound respect because they are a way to God. For the Shakers, work itself was a prayer. If we take the Incarnation seriously, it is not too bizarre to pray blessings over our computers and x-ray machines, calculators and microwaves, all implements through which we express our creativity and help spread God's reign.

Celtic spirituality integrated the mundane into prayer in a way that could enliven our routines. As Esther de Waal writes, "religion both permeated and informed the whole world of life, so that there was no formal distinction between the sacred and the secular, the material and the spiritual. In Scotland, Ireland and Wales centuries ago,... religion did not call men and women out of their environment, but redeemed them within it."[2]

From kindling the fire in the morning to banking it in the evening, the Celtic peoples turned the most monotonous chores into occasions for reverent blessing. Like modern people, they were too busy for long, uninterrupted prayers, so they celebrated each task: milking and churning, brewing ale and bathing. Undergirding their prayer was the belief that we chat with a God who is never far away:

> I on Thy path, O God
> Thou, God, in my steps.

The Korean theologian Chung Hyun-Kyung tells a modern version of the prayer of exorcism. A few years ago, three thousand women who lived in Sri Lanka gathered angrily at the temple of the goddess Kali; their children had disappeared and been murdered by a brutally oppressive government. The mothers ritualized their outrage at these demonic powers. Furiously they smashed coconuts and hurled shells at posters of Sri Lankan dictators. Prayer isn't always sedentary and, under justifiable circumstances, it is anything but placid.

Yet the genius of the variety and diversity is that prayer can also swell with serenity. Sometimes I pray like the woman who made a fragrant pot of herbal tea, wrapped herself in a quilt, listened to Mozart and gazed out her window at the exquisitely tinted evening light lingering and shining on the heights of Pike's Peak. Her worship space was her home; all five of her senses combined for her vespers.

If we think of prayer as a formal activity which occurs only in a distant church, we risk missing the infinite variety it can bring to our days and nights, to our workplaces and to our homes.

Notes

[1] Esther de Waal, *A Seven Day Journey with Thomas Merton* (Ann Arbor, Mich.: Servant Publications, 1992), p. 82.
[2] Esther de Waal, *Every Earthly Blessing: Celebrating a Spirituality of Creation* (Ann Arbor, Mich.: Servant Publications, 1992), p. 14.

PART THREE

❦

Prayerful Juxtapositions

The basis of modern poetry, said poet and critic T. S. Eliot, springs from placing two radically different things in tension. Could that also be true of prayer? Sometimes we are jolted into prayer by strange configurations.

Yet if all is grace, all given by God, it's not so strange. If everything is rooted in the same ground of being, then the springboards to prayer are everywhere. "There is nothing that cannot become a sacramental encounter," said Saint Augustine. So, from grocery stores and butterfly pavilions can spring thanks, petition and praise.

Praying With Photography

So much of my work is tied up with words—writing books, writing articles, writing speeches, writing poems, editing other people's words—that sometimes I long for wordless prayer. What delight when a photograph can prompt a prayer! Somehow it cuts across my usual heady, analytical approach and opens up another side of me. Like music, it is another language—one in which I am less fluent. Nonetheless, I'm eager to learn.

So I sit, surrounded by photos, especially those of lovely scenes. They help me see reality with renewed appreciation. A skilled photographer can capture a scene, even one we have loved, with such careful attention to detail that what we missed in experience we can regain through the photograph.

A favorite picture of autumn woods veiled with fog perfectly expresses the spirit of the season. The simple figures of a stone wall and wooden gate in the foreground anchor the hazy forest in the background. It recalls a day when I realized with a jolt that I had almost missed September. It had been an especially busy month, with a book deadline, several trips and multiple commitments. But to miss September was unthinkable: It was one of my favorite times!

So, late in the month, I skipped one session at a day of prayer and went for a long walk in the autumn foliage. The season mirrored my own stage of life. In many ways I was enjoying rich harvest; the trees' veins of gold were reflected in my life. Two children were already grown and independent, my books were selling well, my career seemed to be progressing. At the same time, there was plenty of lush green: two children still at home, many paths yet untried, many ventures still ahead and unknown.

To look at that photograph of autumn woods helps me recall that hike, even in winter. I understood then what Joyce Rupp had said in talks: Spiritually, we can be in more than one season at once. To continue the season/spirituality link, I gaze at a summer picture of water lilies blooming in one of my favorite spots at our local retreat house. I'd prayed there so often in reality that the photograph could carry me there again. Those floating flowers always reminded me of a central image in T. S. Eliot's "Four Quartets":

> And the pool was filled with water out of sunlight,
> And the lotos rose, quietly, quietly.[1]

In the Buddhist tradition the lotus is an image of contemplation. I loved to start a summer morning simply sitting beside the pond, watching the pastel petals open to the light. It was an image, too, of the soul before God, grace coloring our very essence, but I hesitate to wrap words around the experience. To gaze on the photograph is enough: It all comes back again.

Two photos in my collection have more obvious symbolism. One is a misty green field overhung with green trees. A wooden fence angles down the center. I do not know much about composition, but what I like here is the break in the fence, like a gateway into the meadow. It sings of unexplored spaces and open invitations: "Come see!" I have always suspected that beauty is a door to the sacred; when I see this picture, I know it for sure.

The other doorway picture was taken in Santa Fe. An adobe wall frames a rustic wooden door. Well-worn steps lead up to the door. They are gilded with sunlight from the garden beyond. The door is wide open and inviting; surely it gives entrance to a garden where fountains splash and flowers bloom in a cornucopia of color. We don't know that for sure; we see only the path beckoning. What an image for hope!

Transitions can often be rocky; I'm the first to grumble and fuss about change. Presented with a new opportunity, I stall, fret, cling to security. But the photo reminds me that threshold moments are also numinous: A liminal space can beckon into holy mystery. Trusting the God who has blessed previous transitions gives the confidence to cross the doorsill eagerly. As the photograph suggests, that may be a step into beauty and light.

Other photographs illustrate Scripture concretely. A favorite waterfall scene reminds me: "The water that I will give will become in them a spring of water gushing up to eternal life" (John 4:14). Pictures of individual children remind me that this child—every child—is God's child: The camera lens frames the split-second of recognition. A photograph of a vegetable stand, overflowing with richly shaded produce in purple, jade, crimson, burgundy and earthy clay tones assures me of God's providence, "I will not leave you orphans"; I will always nurture you. Pictures of flowers are mainstays in winter, joyful reminders of resurrection.

Praying with photographs may seem rather formless to people who are used to praying by the book. One standard to apply is, how do I feel after this form of prayer? Meditating with photographs leaves me centered and serene, alert to the mysterious possibilities of other photos that surround me daily. So, for times when books wear thin or I tire of the torrent of words, the photographs stand ready: beautiful, mute, simple, profound.

Notes

[1] T. S. Eliot, "Four Quartets," *Collected Poems* (San Diego: Harcourt, Brace and Company, 1963), p. 176.

A Question of Identity

"Zacchaeus, hurry and come down; for I must stay at your house today." (Luke 19:5)

"[Bartimaeus] Go; your faith has made you well." (Mark 10:52)

"Daughter, your faith has made you well; go in peace, and be healed of your disease." (Mark 5:34)

"Little girl, get up!" (Mark 5:41)

"Woman, where are they? Has no one condemned you?... Neither do I condemn you." (John 8:10-11)

"Lazarus, come out!" (John 11:43)

"Mary." "Teacher!" (John 20:16)

"Then he said to Thomas, 'Put your finger here and see my hands. Reach out your hand and put it in my side....'" (John 20:27)

"Simon son of John, do you love me?" (John 21:16)

It happens over and over: through the look, the greeting, the healing touch. Jesus sees past the appearance, the disease, the blindness, the evil, the skepticism, even the death shroud, to the deeper identity. As John Shea points out, Jesus saw the real, sometimes miserable conditions people were in and didn't blink. But the affliction wasn't absolute; he didn't allow it to dominate his vision. He saw past the debilitating illness or the bitter grief to God's precious child.

More than any other daughter or son of God, Jesus knew this lasting identity and knew that it surpasses any other temporary condition. During the passion, he may have seemed like the victim of stupid cruelty, just as it appeared that Lazarus died tragically young, or Bartimaeus was doomed to blindness, or the woman caught in adultery was permanently tainted by sin. But that wasn't the final answer for any of them; God takes a longer view. What else was Jesus' Resurrection but the victory of God's eternally beloved, chosen child over death itself?

In his typically courteous way, Jesus invites those he encounters to share his convictions. The dynamic recurs often in the Gospels as different people gradually come to know and love in themselves what Jesus saw and loved in them. As it turned out, Peter wasn't a bumbling idiot but a capable leader. Salome the meddlesome mother became a pillar of the early Church. Thomas the doubter would voice a cry of faith that has resounded down the centuries. Zacchaeus wasn't only a greedy tax collector but also an extraordinarily generous man; Martha wasn't a busybody but an insightful theologian; and the little girl who appeared to be dead was only asleep.

Perhaps as they looked into his eyes, they found their best selves.

"He was their original face," says John Shea. Paul echoes that idea: "And all of us, with unveiled faces, seeing the glory of the Lord...are being transformed into the same image" (2 Corinthians 3:18). In one book title, C. S. Lewis alluded to this transitional time as we grow into our full selves: *Till We Have Faces.*

It is a rare and unique moment when we look into another's eyes and catch that glimpse of our true, full identity. The parent holding the newborn child, the lovers recognizing the depth of their feelings for each other, the last, fond look of the dying person: These glances must preview the glad recognition that will come when finally we look into the face of Christ—and see there ourselves. "...[w]hat we will be has not yet been revealed. What we do know is this: when he is revealed, we will be like him, for we will see him as he is" (1 John 3:2).

Jesus' prayer for us was that his joy might be made complete in us (John 17:13). The whole purpose of his life was to expose the grandeur inherent in each of us, to encourage us so that we could do things that surpassed even what he had done! Yet how much time we spend (even in prayer) berating ourselves, regretting our mistakes, rehashing our failures! How much better it might be if our prayer echoed Jesus': "Thank you for crafting me in your image, one like yourself, who bears the 'family resemblance.' Help me to recognize in my life the lines of yours. I praise you for the splendid joy of being human, a sharing of your own joy. Help me to look into the mirror and see the face of Christ."

Pirouette

It is one of the most stunning turnarounds in Scripture. Jesus has just assured a royal official that his son who had been "at the point of death" will live. The man is not one of Christ's disciples; he has no proof of the promise. Yet he starts for home. He goes purely on the strength of Jesus' word. On the way, his servants meet him and bring the good news: The little boy was cured at the exact hour when Jesus had said, "your son will live."

While the skeleton of the story is given in John 4:46-54, it's an intriguing (yes, even prayerful) activity to fill in the details. This Gospel is proclaimed in the fourth week of Lent, the day after we hear about the cure of the man born blind. That's a tip-off: It will contribute more to the theme of deeper seeing.

If I were to dramatize the story, I'd underscore the turning points, which coincide with people seeing at a new level. The royal official must come with a vivid image in mind: the sick child, his cheeks feverish, the life draining rapidly from his small body. He is a man with authority, used to getting things done quickly and efficiently when he gives the command.

Yet this situation is not so easy to fix. And it is dearer to his heart than arranging any royal banquets or troop movements. This is a son whom he clearly loves. This is close to home. We get a hint of the situation's intensity when we consider that the father knows Jesus only by hearsay, yet takes the risk and makes the time to track him down. His formal restraint cannot disguise his urgency: "Sir, come down before my little boy dies."

What Jesus asks him to do is arduous: to retrace his steps, making the long journey back with no fuel but hope. "Go; your son will live." Most of us would badger Jesus with questions. "Well, are you sure? How do you know? That child is the most precious thing in the world to me and he's terribly ill. If anything happened to him...." In our insecurity and worry, we would demand more proof and fret for reassurance. The royal official turns around on the strength of five frail words.

We can only imagine his train of thought as he walks home. Does he question his sanity? Wonder if he should have acted differently? Before he meets his servants, he must ponder long and hard on this man Jesus. To all appearances, he was a simple rabbi; but he was so convincing, the official accepted his word without question. Was it something in his eyes? The conviction of his manner? A compassion that shone clear, even in a brief encounter? If he was an impostor, the man must do some serious explaining to his family. And yet, he believed him....

We have come to expect a pattern of dramatic reversals for people who meet Jesus; some would call them conversions. The extraordinary thing in this story is how Jesus also changes. He begins by dismissing the request, just as he had earlier, in the same city of Cana. There he had initially refused his mother's request to help an embarrassed young couple who ran out of wine. This time, he dismisses those who want signs and wonders as pseudo-believers. They want only the perks, the goodies, not the reality of the person, the granite-hard way of following him.

But something causes Jesus to see the man differently. Perhaps he looks beyond the immediate request, knows the fuller picture. Had it been hard to conceive this child? Had the child's mother died? Did this child have her laugh, her eyes? The request comes in a context which John leaves vague. But that is an invitation to fill in the details, to create our own story around this little family.

Perhaps Jesus knew that story; perhaps he did not. But always he prefers action to theory. In healing the man born blind, he dismissed an academic exercise in which the disciples wonder, "who sinned, this man or his parents?" He turned instead to the earthy reality of clay and spittle to perform the cure. Again, he pivots from the theory ("those who seek signs don't really deserve my intervention") to the pulsing, breathing, anxious human being before him. Urgently, the man repeats his request. In granting it, Jesus shows how generously he can change his mind.

So what's in it for us, who know how often we vacillate, how frequently we change our minds for no good reason? This story of dramatic turnings speaks to all who confront problems too vast to understand. Human beings wrestle with gargantuan dilemmas: If I solve the problem this way, A will get hurt; if I solve it that way, I'll hurt B. We try to gauge what is unfathomable; we bumble through decisions hampered by our inability to see larger dimensions or longer time frames. Like the royal official, we are so used to having powerful forces at our disposal, that we are confused and vulnerable when they don't apply—often in the most important circumstances. One mother, told of her daughter's impending blindness, took her to every specialist in the country. Like any modern-day North American, she was appalled by their limitations: "What do you mean, you can't fix it?"

Perhaps it is in the teeth of such quandaries that we follow the lead of the concerned father. Clearly and forcefully, he presents the situation to Jesus. His respect for Jesus is obvious in the term "sir," also used by the Samaritan woman in the same chapter (John 4:11). In the popular phrase, he "places it in God's hands." With no further ado, no second guessing, he has the courage to trust.

That decision is the first step on the road home. To turn over a terrible problem to Jesus and entrust him with the solution is the way we become at home, at rest with ourselves. Whatever the outcome (which the official does not know as he sets forth), he and we will live in the safe household of a God who cares for us even more than we treasure our most beloved child.

In the most ragged life situations, where answers don't seem to be forthcoming even though years have passed, it may help to remember the royal official. Not seeing the solution, we can still set out for home. What burns in our hearts and what sings in our minds is the promise, "you will live." And somehow, we want to trust him. Somehow we're willing to set aside our knowledge and travel blind.

The Sacramental Principle

Yeah, I know—all is drenched in grace, overflowing with Godhead. But on a dreary day in February, in the midst of the forty-something blizzard of the year, it's hard to remember. Despite what I believe and voice, I still get skeptical. The malaise worsens when the kids have a holiday for no apparent reason other than teacher sanity, anonymous critics ask that I be dis-invited to speaking engagements, and pressing work is neglected because I must find some way to entertain the children and their friends on this miserable day.

My mental state has all the makings for what literary types call a fit of high dudgeon, but actually feels more like dank dungeon. Until, by some amazing grace, the children and I discover the Butterfly Pavilion for our field trip of the day. There, under a glass dome on a snowy prairie, a slice of the tropics flourishes.

The air is warm and moist; mist from a sprinkler system maintains the proper humidity. In this climate, flowers flourish: nuggets of pink-gold lantana; candles of pink blossoms; white petals and crimson clusters. Eyes adjusted to monochromatic winter landscapes blink to grow accustomed to so much green. Feathery ferns, elephant-sized leaves, equatorial vegetation flourish beside a stream filled with fish undulating in the colors of the Caribbean.

While I do not understand the scientific technicalities, I appreciate the fact that this wild jungle creates the proper home for butterflies. They are everywhere; the air palpitates with their presence. One as spotted as a black-and-white dalmatian drinks deeply from a red chalice of flowery nectar. Here one lights on a woman's purse; there another rests on a child's head. Earth-toned ones anchor on tree bark, dark brown eyes the centers of their wings. Others drag a weight of beauty in their wings: trains of paisley as gloriously jeweled as any king's or queen's.

If stripes can take flight, they are here: fluttering on the air, yellow and black. They cluster around the windows, lattices like stained glass vibrant against the snow. They descend like surprises on the children whose faces look up, rapt. Such reverent stillness falls over these children that their parents, used to more action, might not recognize them. As if playing statue, they wait in anticipation, arms outstretched for a landing so light they barely feel it.

My own daughter is absorbed in watching a butterfly whose outer wings are a dull brown, but whose inner wings are a startling, iridescent blue. Each flutter reveals the secret core, the hidden azure, just as each wave of the sea can unveil another tone. A guide notices her fascination and comments, "That's a common morpho."

"*Common?*" she asks in utter disbelief. I want to cheer her; it is the same thought I had left unexpressed. While the guide rattles on about this type being common in El Salvador, I'm off on another mental channel. Recently, I'd heard Michael Himes from Boston College describe his concept of sacramentality: "That which is always and everywhere true must be noticed, acknowledged and celebrated somewhere, sometime."

Himes points out that what is always the case is frequently ignored—how often do we register a heartbeat or count the blinks of the eye? Because grace is everywhere, because we live always in the constant love of the gracious God, it takes a conscious effort to recognize this presence. Anything that helps us notice is a sacrament with a small *s*. Through the jungle-under-glass I carry Saint Augustine's words, "There is nothing that cannot become a sacramental encounter."

The truth of his statement becomes clear at the next stop, the chrysalis cage. Hundreds of them are pinned to a wall, some pulsing with movement, others withered skins from which the life has already flown. Here for the first time, the radiant wings unfold. The curator who slides open the window has long, slender fingers that handle a butterfly so precisely that he can sometimes slip three between the fingers of one hand.

Gently, he then carries a flock of these newborns to their

release in the pseudo-jungle. A crowd of children and adults surround him as he explains which ones are still too "soft" to fly; gently he attaches these to a tree branch. Others are ready to launch; they fly onto clothing and people, creating a man's bow tie on his shirt, a girl's ribbon on her hair. The faces surrounding the "butterfly man" (does he have a title?) fill with delight.

People take pictures in a futile attempt to capture the wonder, but this is a moment to receive with open palms. Fragile and lacy, the wings alight briefly, unpredictably. Theological language seems cumbersome, but only its phrases can rise to the occasion: Standing on holy ground, we glimpse the sacred.

Did the scene echo Eden? In that garden, God and humans were equally convinced that "it was good." So it was in the Butterfly Pavilion where we relished that original vision of Yahweh. Deep as a breath of fragrant air, light as a stroke of wing, beautiful as fluttering topaz and jade, all created for our delight.

Grocery Store Prayer

A friend of mine delights in the fruit and vegetable section of the grocery store. The wide array of colors, textures, tastes and smells speak to her of God's abundance. I agree. When we don't race through, it's a feast for the senses: the smooth purple of eggplant beside the pale blush of apricots; feathery greens near strawberries glowing like rubies. But I have come to appreciate another aspect of my weekly visit: the quietly cheerful employees.

They may never attend a religious education convention or read the latest works of spiritual writers. Yet they epitomize the "liturgy of the world," Karl Rahner's term for God's continual self-communication, the transcendent mediated by the dailiness of life. We do not relate to an aloof, distant God, but one who is close, transforming us by grace.

The produce man has probably not read Rahner. Yet I learn compassion from him as he engages almost daily in the same conversation with the same woman. She dresses up for grocery shopping: heels, plaid skirt, navy blazer, matching bow in her hair. One would think she was off to a corporate board meeting or an executive office instead of the lettuce aisle. Having observed this phenomenon several times, I feel safe in saying it's a habit. She queries the produce man about the freshness of the broccoli; they engage in intense discussion about the ripeness of the pears. I suspect it is the only conversation she has all day. He is kind enough to take it seriously; his comments about bananas seem reflective. Every time I observe surreptitiously, I pray that when I'm old and lonely, God will send me an understanding produce man.

At the checkout stands, elderly shoppers are warmly greeted by their first names. It is a social ritual as the checkers inquire about their health, their activities, their relatives. Major diplomacy ensues as the checkers balance the needs of the loquacious against the grumbles of those waiting in line behind them. They have a sure instinct for who needs a few extra minutes to describe their flu symptoms and who is running short on food stamps this week.

Their courtesy seems extraordinary for people who have probably been on their feet all day and who are not making a huge salary. In other offices today, the well-to-do are paying large sums of money for the attentive ears of professional counselors. Far more moving is the modestly paid checker who engulfs a frail old woman in a huge embrace, and clucks, "You get to the doctor, now, hear? I'm worried about you not taking your medicine, honey...."

Of course, this store has its share of surly clerks and its "just get the job done" types. But there are a few here who illustrate for me the sanctity of ordinary people.

Most are not overly educated; certainly none are on the national lecture circuit. Periodically, they seem to be honored with "Employee of the Month" or some other badge of recognition, but that only skims the surface. They should be canonized, their virtues proclaimed from cathedrals.

In his biographical account of the late Jesuit author William Lynch, David Toolan, S.J., tells of the sure instincts of the kind of person we might be tempted to take for granted: a hospital aide. No poems are written about such people; few homilists mention them. But they bring the world salt and light.

It seems that when Father Lynch was dying in a New York hospital, he would explore imaginatively the territory that lay ahead of him. Intently, he would invite his nurse to join him on his mental travels. The literal-minded nurse would rebuke him and feed him fantasy: "Father Lynch, you're not going anywhere; you're going to get well...." He knew she was patronizing him and he would have none of it.

But the nurse's aide understood. "I'll come, Father," she'd reply cheerily. "I'm ready when you are." That was all he needed; he'd reenter his imaginative exploration with a big grin.[1]

How little we sometimes need. How easy it is to provide. How many opportunities we miss. Odd insights to accumulate along with the groceries. But the willingness of ordinary people to offer ordinary kindness can be a kind of nurture. I leave the store uplifted, whistling softly to myself.

Notes

[1] David Toolan, "Some Biographical Reflections on William F. Lynch's Thought," in Sandra Yocum Mize and William Portier, eds., *American Catholic Traditions: Resources for Renewal*. Annual Publication of the College Theology Society, Vol. 42 (Maryknoll, N.Y.: Orbis Books, 1997), pp. 134-135.

Foundering in a Blizzard

Sometimes an experience jolts us out of ourselves and into the "beyond," that sphere that isn't controlled by our automatic behaviors and knee-jerk responses. Sometimes it's a brush with death or a startling glimpse of beauty. Sometimes it's a friend's unexpected comment, or an experience surpassing our habitual range. This time it was a blizzard.

Nasty snowstorms strike Colorado just as it's poised on the edge of spring. A few warm days bring out tiny leaves on the trees; the lilac buds begin to uncoil. We relax in the warmth, feeling as privileged as residents of warmer climates. Who needs a Caribbean cruise when we have Colorado sunshine? Then it strikes: the March blizzard, even more pernicious because our guard is down.

We forget, from year to year. We get our shorts out of storage and buy spring colors, indulge in pastel shoes when it's more likely we'll be wearing boots on Easter. So I dismissed the snowflake or two falling lazily one morning in late March. I had appointments to keep, places to be! No light snowfall could deter me—and besides, how bad could it get when the temperature had reached 76 degrees the day before?

Pretty bad. I cursed my stupidity several hours later. I had plenty of time to reflect on my naïveté while stuck on the highway for two hours. A driving wind screamed around the car and the snow pelted the windshield. Huge rigs jackknifed across the road, making it impassable. The wipers, fighting an icy glacier on the windshield, went haywire and refused to clear a space for vision. As I battled with an ice scraper stuck out the side window, I berated myself. What had been so important that I couldn't postpone? Why was I doing this? And worst of all, was my family worried?

The last question stung the most, perhaps because I've spent a major part of motherhood worrying over offspring driving through similarly dangerous conditions. When they'd finally tumble through the door, I'd ask frostily, "so—no phones anywhere?" Now, with restricted visibility, I couldn't sight a filling station. I was afraid that if I found one and left the highway to telephone, I'd never be able to get back on the road. I was playing out the same scenario about which I'd given so many dire warnings.

To telescope an arduous afternoon, I finally collapsed safely before the fireplace at home with a large cup of tea and a larger sense of gratefulness. Though I've read it and even written about it, only a direct experience convinces me that in my weakness is my strength. Only when I let the defenses down and become vulnerable, even intensely stupid, do I appreciate saving grace. It would not be an overstatement to say that every cell tingled with gratitude. Over and over, I thanked God for such magnificent graciousness to one of such obviously limited intelligence. Thanks pulsed through me: that I had not been harmed and my family had not suffered. Before I regressed to the anesthesia of "normalcy," I wanted to bow low in praise, sing wonder and thanks to God.

The dance in the fire, the tulip tips now covered by snow, the swirl of the flakes, the surge of wind: You drive it all, O God. And what of me? You say we humans are worth more than the chorus of sparrows now making a din beneath the eaves despite the snow. My ignorance may have great depth, but even larger is the space you sculpt within me to fill with your praise.

No other creature has the capacity to reflect on an experience and draw meaning from it. The deer probably burrowed deeper into the underbrush, the rabbits hunkered into their nests. Tomorrow they will forage in the sunlight, the cold forgotten.

And I, warm and close to my hearth now? Only the human can create from near-misfortune a springboard to prayer. As the weather newscasts grow grimmer and the accident toll rises, I can turn to you in thanks. Saved from the blizzard and my own stupidity, I should write a psalm, dance to tambourines, unfurl a crimson banner, lift golden vessels wafting aromatic incense.

Instead, I offer you the imperfect gift of my tattered trust. Once again, I have glimpsed your providence. Unseen, you have walked with me. You have shown me once more how you delight in me and guard me, press on beside me, hem me round with care. This time, let me learn the lesson by heart.

The Morning After: Safe Harbor

"We forget what we need to remember, and remember what we need to forget."[1] I nodded in agreement when I came across this sentence. How often my thoughts are cluttered with the negative: I remember a slight and forget a thousand compliments. One downward turn grates in the mind when a hundred miles of soaring upwards lie as rusty and neglected as old airplane parts. As I try to be more alert to those things which should be remembered, I savor this experience and hope it is engraved on the long-term memory.

The morning after a nasty March blizzard, I awaken to crystal clear skies and the return of warm weather. Such surprises evoke one response: a walk outdoors before breakfast. Hugging a steaming red coffee mug, I carve the first set of tracks through the snow. It is probably a cliché to say that it glistened like a carpet of diamonds, but that is the perfect description for the pillows of prisms on which I walked.

The irony did not escape me: Yesterday the snow led to an arduous drive and a stressful afternoon. Yesterday, I was afraid. Today, this same stuff has created beauty and wonderment. It coats the world with a shiny glaze; it softens all the rough edges; it cloaks the earth in a peaceful sheen where before was only brown clay. The symbolism almost shouts: That which I first fear may be deceptive. The suspicious visitor may bring surprising gifts.

How that paradox is borne out by the Christian tradition! Throughout Scripture, marginalized people bring stunning insights; sometimes the ostracized Gentile sees more clearly than the Jew with Abraham's birthright—the sure ticket to salvation. Certainly this was true in Christ's life: The apparent disaster on Calvary became our glorious salvation. Through the blood of the martyrs, tortured, shamed and humiliated, comes the inspiration of the whole people.

It is one thing to have that knowledge in the head, another to experience it in the body. So I walked with care over that ivory carpet. I sang to myself the beautiful Celtic hymn, "The Deer's Cry":

> I arise today
> Through the strength of heaven
> Light of sun
> Radiance of moon
> Splendor of fire
> Speed of lightning
> Swiftness of wind
> Depth of the sea
> Stability of earth
> Firmness of rock
>
> I arise today
> through God's strength to pilot me
> God's eye to look before me
> God's wisdom to guide me
> God's way to lie before me
> God's shield to protect me....

It was a prayer of pure praise. It could only have happened in this setting, at this unique time of year when winter and spring balance on the same threshold.

I tried to imprint on my senses the profound truth: What looks like a curse can turn to blessing. Will I remember it the next time a crisis rears its ugly head? Like any limited human, I'll probably fly into a dither again, waste hours on worry, fret over things I cannot change. But if I am fortunate, the grace of this "morning after" will return and remind me. Delay judgment; wait 'til the final chapter is in. Over and over, the problems and frustrations raise the question in our lives, "Who will separate us from the love of Christ?" (Romans 8:35).

Paul continues, "Will hardship, or distress, or persecution, or famine, or nakedness, or peril, or sword?" Ignatius would look for the other face of the problem: "How is this crisis creating me? How is this event, however painful, another opportunity for God's entry?" We may all answer in different ways, but my answer today came as lightly and easily as snowfall: Nothing can drive us from Christ. "For I am convinced that neither death, nor life, nor angels, nor rulers, nor things present, nor things to come, nor powers, nor height, nor depth, nor anything else in all creation, will be able to separate us from the love of God in Christ Jesus our Lord" (Romans 8:38-39).

Notes

[1] Don Richard Riso, *Enneagram Transformations* (Boston: Houghton Mifflin, 1993), p. 115.

Moved by Art

Thank you, Wendy Beckett! I have never seen the Carmelite nun whose BBC television series *Sister Wendy's Odyssey* has been widely acclaimed. But two of her books (I look forward to more), *Meditations on Joy* and *The Gaze of Love* have brought me not only a new way of seeing, but a new way of praying.

In her introduction to the latter book, she explains that she usually avoids focusing on overtly religious art because it could suggest that Jesus lived in "fancy dress times" and that we need a special language such as ancient Latin to talk with God.

Already she is on my wavelength!

But before following that track, I must pause for her exception, the one religious painting she analyzes. Discussing a painting by Guercino of the woman taken in adultery, she focuses on the hands of Jesus, who gestures toward the woman with "infinite understanding." His tenderness contrasts with the hands of the accuser, who points at her as though she were an object, "a 'thing' on which to hang his theology."[1]

Sister Wendy then describes Jesus in a way that is both startling and touching. "He is the only man who has looked into the cloud, seen with His own eyes the Face of the holy mystery, and turned round to assure us that the name of God is 'Father.'"[2] How true. If I had the chance to gaze into the eyes of the Father, I suspect I'd be lost there, so absorbed in beauty and compassion that nothing could make me turn around. (It's hard enough to pull my attention away from a good book!) Yet Jesus did, foregoing his own delighted rest in order to reassure us. This insight places him in a new light that helps me to love him more.

She then turns to a subject more typical for her, the world of modern art, which can affect us with raw emotion "even before we have our reverence ready."[3] She not only appreciates art; she writes with humor and skill! I am especially interested in the parallels she draws between art and prayer. A picture of an athlete walking through a meadow shows how we, too, can bend our psychic energies into prayer. Just as the walker seems to be drawn magnetically to a goal, so are we drawn by grace to God. And—great consolation—our poor attempt is never wasted.

In Ken Kiff's painting "Man Greeting Woman" Sister Wendy interprets the two naked creatures as symbolic of our stance before God. When we enter resolutely into Jesus, she promises, we can be stripped of accretions and become as infantile, vulnerable and shrimp-pink as the nudes in the painting. "It is a picture of total trust," she explains.[4]

The older I get, the more grateful I am for wordless prayer forms. An image such as this one can flash into my day with a directness that complex language lacks. When my schedule bogs me down in detail, I can remember Martha Alf's pears, drawn in the simplest of media with the greatest attention. Caressed by light, their pale, rounded forms call us to look more closely at the many other objects of beauty we overlook in an ordinary day. Carrying a mental image like a talisman can shift perspective in subtle but important ways. It can also speak when we are too tired, too busy or too frustrated to muster words.

Lest prayer ever become dour drudgery, Sister Wendy restores its joy. She reminds us that joy is sterner than happiness and flashes on us with a transforming suddenness that our usual "settled cheerfulness"[5] cannot approach. In "a snatched moment of sensuous celebration,"[6] we can glimpse one of joy's hallmarks: "absolute belief in what is experienced."[7] If this sounds abstract, she calls attention to the details: the light glinting on rich meadows, food and wine, the peace of folded hands, dazzling color.

The paintings, with their brilliant tones and sculpted forms, suggest what no canvas can contain; they recall for us our own experiences of joy. We can gaze on Borgognone's saint and, though we may not relate to the religious habit or seventeenth-century setting, nod in agreement. "Ah, yes. I've been there," we say to ourselves and smile slightly. We recognize her rapt expression, the graceful folds of her clothes, the buoyancy of her posture. The art sets up a resonance, between us and it, between us and the divine. Doesn't that connection set us squarely on the path to prayer?

Notes

1. Sister Wendy Beckett, *The Gaze of Love* (San Francisco: HarperSanFrancisco, 1994), p. 18.
2. Ibid.
3. Ibid., p. 19.
4. Ibid., p. 64.
5. Sister Wendy Beckett, *Meditations on Joy* (New York: DK Publishing, Inc., 1995), 8.
6. Ibid., p. 12.
7. Ibid., p. 14.

PART FOUR

⸎

Given Moments

God, who seeks always to be in dialogue with us, can use unpredictable ways to start the conversation. Because grace permeates everything, a wide range of places, people, experiences and times can lead us through the doorway of prayer.

Anyone who has been separated from a loved one can appreciate the experience. Our memory is stirred by the smallest encounters: a perfume, a favorite food, a snatch of music, a line of poetry. Suddenly, a face flashes before us; the beloved person is vivid in the mind. Defying distances of time and space, we come together again. Such a joyous reunion reveals the wonder of prayer: We are together again with God.

Travel Prayer

"Flight 77 now departing from Gate C-3." Am I the only one who hears that familiar announcement as a call to prayer? To many folks, travel represents dreary motels, holding patterns and plastic food. I claim it as unique opportunity.

Travel gives the everyday a fresh-scrubbed, morning face. New places and people have a sheen, a newness, an abundant energy lacking in familiar routines. Experience on a trip has a special edge: the surety that when the homebound flight takes off at 11:19 from Concourse C, everything left undone and unsaid will remain so. It's a lot like life: no second chances, no dress rehearsals. This is it.

On a recent trip, the whistle of the homebound train echoed an image from Anne Tyler's *Dinner at the Homesick Restaurant*: "He had missed an opportunity. It was like missing a train—or something more important, something that would never come again. There was no explanation for the grief that suddenly filled him."[1]

Travel intensifies our intuition that everything is on loan. Like library books that eventually must be returned, challenges and chances are offered once. Knowing the due date, I live with more awareness and clarity. I taste the tart and the sweet; I savor the beach knowing I'll soon be back in the blizzard. I may not see my long-distance friend for another five years, so I relish our rare conversations.

I also gain a new perspective on life back home: what is askew, what is cherished. Travel allows a fresh start. Robert Frost had this vision when he climbed his favorite birch tree:

> I'd like to get away from earth a while
> And then come back to it and begin over....[2]

Recently, when I traveled to a hot-spring pool, I realized that my swimming strokes were not really necessary to keep me afloat. The wonderful buoyancy of the water held me. That trip taught me something about trust, in the clear, graphic way images communicate.

From the purely practical standpoint, travel offers a temporary suspension of all the details that weigh me down. When I'm not trying to figure out a jiffy way to camouflage leftover pot roast, or hunting for two minutes to finish filing three remaining fingernails, it's liberating in a spiritual sense. Certain that I can stay seated throughout breakfast, I can inhale the warm fragrance of my blueberry muffin. Knowing that no child will interrupt, I can start reading a novel. I can fully enjoy the daisies when I'm not burdened by their care. Someone else's weeding and watering gives me the chance to take the "long, loving look at the real" that is contemplation.

In a new setting, I needn't argue, analyze or describe. I can enter in. Wonderfully unhurried, unpressured by the usual domestic and job constraints, I can see with my whole self. The stultifying routine is interrupted; I can indulge my latent capacity for exploration. A new hiking trail? park? museum? lake? I am completely engaged. No one in this city knows me; no one phones; no one cares about my uncoordinated clothes. Not bound by utility or convention, I can soar in unexpected ways and savor the surprises. The sense of play which is vital to contemplation thrives in an unfamiliar locale.

When God wanted a word with the people of Scripture, God called them to the desert. That vast solitude set the scene for extraordinary revelations. Even though I board a jumbo jet, I see my travels in the same light. "Give up what you are," God invites, "to discover what you can become." The journey metaphor for the spiritual life may be overused, but it still contains seeds of truth. When I am far from home with its usual comfort and props, I am more conscious of my ultimate vulnerability, my absolute reliance on God.

Walter Burghardt, S.J., speaks of a world thirsting for people who know and love God personally. If these thirsty people touch me and do not thrill to the touch, they abide in loneliness, in the terrible absence of God. If I come across as one who has not looked long enough and hard enough at the real, I fail them.

So I take the chances and rise to the challenges that travel presents. The agent keeping track of my frequent-flier miles probably doesn't guess the hidden agenda of my trips. But I have found the skies friendly, and the path beckoning to the heart of God.

Notes

[1] Anne Tyler, *Dinner at the Homesick Restaurant* (New York: Knopf, 1982).
[2] Robert Frost, "Birches," in Richard Abcarian and Marvin Klotz, eds. *Literature: The Human Experience* (New York: St. Martin's Press, 1984), p. 74.

Prayer in Cramped Places

"How can I pray when I'm constantly driving, working, cooking, doing laundry or picking up toys?" My friend's question touched a familiar chord. I, too, feel trapped in a spiral of constant activity that leaves little space or time for quiet, uninterrupted prayer. To most busy people of our century, long hours filled with contemplation are relics of an earlier, unhurried era. Yet we still hunger for the depth and meaning prayer can bring our frantic days.

Perhaps the answer lies in wordless prayer, gestures and images that can fit between stop signs or can fill the mind and heart as we unload the dishwasher. Such prayer does not require the long process of centering, nor a hasty search for book or Bible; we simply sink into God for a few peaceful minutes.

We can turn to these forms when we are exhausted, annoyed, distracted, depressed or busy. One morning I was so tired I tried to heat my coffee in the refrigerator instead of the microwave. I was grateful then to Joyce Rupp, O.S.M., for a sequence of gestures to start the day in grace, no matter how groggy I am. I begin by raising both arms to heaven (also a welcome stretch for a crotchety spine). That reach thanks the Creator for the gift of another day. Then I extend both arms outwards horizontally to symbolize compassion with all humankind. The next gesture is opening and cupping my hands. The motion speaks of willingness to receive whatever surprises God may send today. Finally, both arms crossed over the heart say, "I will spend this day with you, God and Friend."

Throughout the day those early morning gestures resonate. A whiff of perfume, a favorite song on the radio, a compliment? Ah—remember the cupped hands. A call from a friend in pain recalls the gesture of solidarity. A difficult situation at work? I approach it in grace.

Like the gestures, the images of prayer can grace unexpected places. Curtis Bryant, S.J., writes in *Orphaned Wisdom*:

...God loves life
in its failure
as much as in its
fruitfulness.[1]

The image that reminds me of God's broad acceptance is our family at dinner. Don't think for a minute that it's the placid, psalmist's scene of olive plants around the table. The phone is ringing, the rolls are burning, and someone is rushing off to a meeting. One child sulks over a poor grade; another exults because he made the soccer team. One daughter twirls a lovely braid of auburn hair, while another laments the odd effect of over-plucking her eyebrows. Throughout the meal, I inconsistently dispense criticism and heap praise. ("Use a napkin, not the tablecloth!" "You finished your homework—yeah!") When failure and fruitfulness sit close enough to pass the potato salad, I praise the God who created this scene.

Michael Moynahan, S.J., draws another image in the same book. He describes a giant oak tree with its branches reaching out:

Together,
one mighty,
open palm of praise.[2]

Now when I see winter branches scraping the sky, I think of the hand of God. In spring, the branches cradle birds. When tempted to panic, I remember that palm holding me.

Attending a talk recently, I was struck by one thought in it: We live in temporary shelter, but always dwell richly in the embrace of God. I realized the full truth of that image later in the week when I traveled to a convention. A friend and I had decided to stay at an inexpensive motel, but I began to realize *why* it was so cheap when I saw the cinder-block walls and brownish-green camouflage-colored bedspreads. Hearing the people next door screaming curses, I imagined rapists in the hall and drug dealers in the parking lot. With fear and trembling, I phoned my friend. He invited me to his room and met me with a reassuring hug. Then all the tawdriness faded, the flutter of fear quieted and we could laugh together.

In a way, we always dwell in temporary shelter. Yet the presence of God can make every dwelling a home. Knowing God's faithfulness helps tame the worst situation and allows us to see its humor and transience. Despite chaos and fear, the God of the large embrace abides always.

Notes

[1] Curtis Bryant, in Michael Moynahan, S.J., *Orphaned Wisdom: Meditations for Lent* (Mahwah, N.J.: Paulist Press, 1990), pp. 53-54.
[2] Moynahan, p. 15.

Clouds and Cracks

An early morning flight on a mosquito-sized airplane helps me see the frailty of the human constructions we lay upon chaos and mystery, trying to control the unfathomable. If you travel as much as I do, you're constantly adjusting your schedule as time slips in and out of different zones. Then just when you think you've got it straightened out, Daylight Savings Time comes along. The changes could have a dizzying effect but, on this trip, I've begun to see them as cracks in our carefully constructed facades.

How often I've felt the stress of too much work, too little time, or longed for another hour or two in a day. How I've rushed to be on time, or created maneuvers to kill a little extra time. With this insight, it all seems laughable. We Anglos especially, who live with one eye on the watch, need this playful reminder that time is not absolute; many things are more important. It's almost as if the hands on the clock, usually stationary and precise, are waving and clapping.

So, too, with perspective. Over the airport hangs a slate grey sky, flat and bleak. But like the clock, it's not the final reality it might first seem. As the plane climbs 26,000 feet, its silver wings cut cleanly through filmy clouds, as though appearances could so easily be shredded. At this altitude, against a cobalt sky rear mountain ranges of clouds— Rockies, Appalachians and Himalayas, studded with Grand Canyons. They are sculpted from puff instead of granite, like soap bubbles or shampoo.

It's nothing new to speak of the perspective gained from flying. Taking her first flight in aviation's pioneering days, Karen Blixen wrote, "so this was it. Now I see and understand everything." In the film version of her story, *Out of Africa*, Meryl Streep simply reaches forward for a silent squeeze of pilot Robert Redford's hand.

In Sheldon Vanauken's *A Severe Mercy*, two young lovers fill the cockpit of their plane with lilacs. Then as the plane swoops and loops into the dawn, blossoms stream back in their wake. The wife calls her husband, "my golden one," and years later when she lies dying, repeats that name. He comments, "I knew all she was remembering: lilacs and flight into the mystery of the dawning and me standing there in the light."[1]

John Shea proposes that Jesus gained the same kind of perspective when he climbed the mountain to proclaim the Beatitudes. Looking at the people from that height, he could see that poverty and grief didn't have the final say. He didn't deny the harsh realities of people's lives, but he kept his sights on God's daughter or son. That identity cannot be diminished, no matter how threatening the circumstances. The outer person might present a sad, decrepit shell, but Jesus saw beneath the surface to the blessedness within. The theme of the Beatitudes is, "Do not make absolute your present state; do not forget the underlying blessedness."

When I was in college, Shakespeare taught me the gaping difference between appearance and reality; now an airplane ride reinforces the message. Perhaps the distinction is also captured by William Lynch, author of *Christ and Apollo* and *Images of Hope*. This Jesuit priest spent a lifetime studying the imagination. As his own death approached, he tried for a realistic imagination, one which "stays with the facts, all the hospital facts," rather than succumb to the culture of denial.[2]

At the same time, he followed Christ, whose own death was simultaneously a passage into nothingness and a movement to life. As Lynch lay dying, he imagined the journey ahead as a trip, "not so much vertically 'up there'; as ahead, in the unknown future."[3]

His image has special significance after my voyage through cloud country and shifting time. How much is beyond us, utterly incomprehensible? Could death itself be such a scrim, seeming so final, but in reality, merely a gauzy veil between us and those who have died? Could the limits we place on reality be false, easily upset by a change in time or altitude or perspective? That might make some people feel insecure, but to others, it's a marvelous invitation past the appearance, into unfolding layers of unguessed reality.

Notes

[1] Sheldon Vanauken, *A Severe Mercy* (San Francisco: Harper & Row, 1977), p. 40.

[2] William Lynch, "Death as Nothingness," *Continuum* 5 (Fall, 1967), pp. 459-469.

[3] David Toolan, "Some Biographical Reflections," pp. 134-135.

Sometimes It Takes a Hurricane

Earlier that summer we'd arrived at Mesa Verde just after lightning hit; eight hundred acres were aflame, and our hotel was being evacuated. Now the three workshops I was scheduled to do in Raleigh, North Carolina, coincided with Hurricane Fran. As I packed, I scanned three-inch headlines about destruction estimated at a billion dollars. According to the newspaper, the city had no power, no water, no phone and no airline service.

It didn't seem like the most opportune time for talks on lectionary-based catechesis. Yet the airline assured me they'd fly, and frantic phone calls to Raleigh produced only taped messages about "technical difficulties." Mustering my courage, I wheeled my suitcase to the front door and waited for the airport shuttle.

Ten minutes before it was scheduled to come, the phone rang. "Don't go!" the office receptionist warned. "Only one lady in the parish has a phone; she called to tell you everything's been canceled."

The relief that flowed over me relaxed all the tension I didn't realize I'd been accumulating. The closest sensation I could compare it to was sliding deep into a hot tub, feeling its warmth spread over aching neck and shoulders.

The utterly unexpected gift of three whole days reminded me of what writer Raymond Carver called the latter part of his life. Diagnosed with a terminal illness, he lived ten years longer than he expected to, and called those years "pure gravy." Recently, due to improved medications, some AIDS patients have been given more time than they anticipated. Such beneficence is like winning the lottery with a prize that for many people, is more precious than money: time. My experience, though a microcosm of these, helped me appreciate the joy of the windfall.

Every moment of that weekend seemed gilded, underscored by the thought: This is time I'm not supposed to have. In one way, I squeezed in a few tasks that, undone, had been annoying me, but I'd simply not had time to get around to. The funny thing about those little demons is how long we allow them to build up, convinced we can't fit them in, yet how quickly they're resolved. In less than an hour, I'd cleaned out a briefcase, trying not to berate myself for the valentines I was carrying around in September, and the memos from early last year, still haunting me late this year. Almost as quickly, I filtered through an annoying pile of clutter on my desk, restoring a clean surface on which I could resume work without distractions.

While that rewarded my *Good Housekeeping* self (albeit a minuscule part of the personality), a far greater part relished beauties I would have missed. The sunset that evening, after a day of rain, glowed with unusual vibrance: Clouds brushed with gold bordered a pure blue patch of sky, like some baroque frame surrounding a picture of the Assumption. Dinner in front of the fire was particularly cozy in contrast with the airplane fare I would have been consuming. Simply moving around the house was a pleasant sensation, as I thought, "I'm not frozen into the same seat for six hours, with all my limbs paralyzed!" Renting a movie, sleeping in my own bed, joking with my children: all these minor pleasures took on new radiance. Critically ill people consider themselves "on borrowed time"; I had that same feeling without the edginess. I was conscious of living "on blessed time."

Which, when we think about it, all time is. To draw breath, walk on green grass, digest food, sleep deeply: whoever said we deserved these gifts? Whoever merited one moment of life? Yet here it is: all given, with special plums like beauty and laughter thrown into the bargain.

I am scheduled for ten more trips before next summer's hiatus. Most of them will run like clockwork: flights, shuttles, hotels, gracious audiences, parts of the world I've never seen waiting to be discovered, business contacts to make. Usually I enjoy the stimulation and look forward to the next trip. But how much I've learned from the one-in-a-million cancellation! How rich this time removed from time.

Scrambled Eggs and the Baptism of Jesus

One Sunday before breakfast, I read John Kavanaugh's reflections on the baptism of Jesus in *The Word Encountered*. He addresses the controversy: Why did Jesus need baptism if he was sinless? And, if Jesus did not sin, was he really like us, fully human?

A tough dilemma for one who has not yet had coffee. Yet Kavanaugh resolves it expertly, explaining that to misunderstand Jesus' baptism is to misunderstand our humanity. Christ came to reveal us to ourselves, to enter fully into what it means to be human. "Our sin is nothing other than the rejection of the truth of our humanity."[1] Jesus shows us our true face, ourselves at our best. "He accepts full solidarity with us even if it means being seen as sinner."[2]

What heartening words. He is like me; I am like him. I'm sure I've heard it before, but the truth strikes with particular force in this chilly kitchen, with sun glinting off the snow outside the window. I feel affirmed in all that I am, the messy parts as well as the better ones, because Jesus became one of us. Long before anyone measured I.Q., analyzed us with Myers-Briggs or slotted our personality types on the enneagram, Jesus embraced the whole lot—introverts and extroverts, sensates and intuitives, thinkers and feelers, crusaders and artists—the whole kit and caboodle.

To such a stunning act of generosity, how does one respond? I suppose each person's answer would be different. But I resolve to enter more fully into my humanity, savoring it as he did. Specifically, that means life as a layperson, a mother and wife. I have many friends who are vowed religious and recently spent several days on retreat with them. But the contrast of our life-styles only serves to heighten my appreciation for who I am called to be.

My family still sleeps in the Sunday quiet, but I think of each member with fondness. Then I do something I have not done in quite a while. I prepare a huge breakfast which, with our heightened cholesterol consciousness, we do not eat often. Somehow, it seems fitting to celebrate the baptism of Jesus with scrambled eggs and bacon, cinnamon rolls, hot chocolate and fragrant coffee. When the family emerges, drowsy and wrinkled in their flannel pajamas and robes, they will feast.

Like most moms, I cook many meals in a frenzy. With hungry hordes at my back, I whiz through a routine learned over a quarter century. Whip out those plates, pour that juice, get the show on the road. It is hardly a contemplative moment.

But here in the Sunday silence, free of pressure, I cook more reflectively. I remember Teresa of Avila saying that the height of her prayer was learning to watch an egg fry. I don't become eloquent about stirring yolks and whites. But I do so with an awareness of an opportunity to nurture my family on a cold morning. It is a chance none of my religious friends have. It is our particular path to the holy, right here at home.

Later in the morning, we take another path, to church. With the frigidity of the subzero temperatures that day, our worship space seems particularly inviting. People leave their coats on for Mass, joke about the weather and create a warmth simply in their bulky gathering. Ah, this is what he meant. This is the humanity Jesus entered and loved.

A reminder of our baptism comes as we are sprinkled liberally with water from a pine branch. The children giggle; adults previously focused on the cold weather are startled by the drops on their skin. It calls me to do what Christ did: enter deeply into what is uniquely mine. Too often I try end runs around my humanity. I attempt to overcome my limitations, run faster, do more, ignore my body and zoom over buildings faster than a speeding bullet. In an era that exalts "Supermom," it's not an empty temptation.

Yet Jesus seems to be calling us into something utterly different: a simple appreciation of the beauty of this human state, with all its weaknesses and sorrows. When we enter into it as he did, we look with new eyes on old sources of strength—family, home, church, scrambled eggs on Sunday morning.

Notes

[1] John Kavanaugh, *The Word Encountered* (Maryknoll, N.Y.: Orbis Books, 1996), p. 16.
[2] Kavanaugh, p. 16.

Prayerful Pauses

Usually the process called "faith sharing" makes me nervous. Where in that phrase is there room for doubt, for uncertainty, for the presence of God so elusive no conversation can pin it down? My kind of spirituality is more comfortable with mystery than with intimate revelations around the coffee or conference table. I also worry about the possibility of one-upsmanship at such gatherings. Would one person's mysticism lead to another's visions or levitation?

So of course, as with many other good things, I was snookered into faith sharing unwittingly. I turned up for a meeting; it turned out that "faith sharing" was first on the agenda. With no means of escape, I burrowed into the cookies and coffee, figuring I'd ride it out in sulky silence. The God of surprises must have delighted in the fact that, five minutes later, I was deeply engaged and—rare for an introvert—vocal.

As it turned out, this was no place for pious platitudes or arrogance. The people around the table were busy; they held positions of responsibility; they wrestled with the questions of faith in the marketplace, the hospital, the giant corporation. So we struggled with finding God in the messiness: How could actions which led to long chains of evil be instigated by surprisingly good people? How did we find God by inaction as well as by action? How could one maintain any semblance of a spiritual life in the onslaught of constant demands and pressures?

We discussed the gospel passage of two brothers, asked by their father to go into the field. One said no, but went later. Another said yes, but didn't go. How were our uses of "yes" and "no" all tangled together so that sometimes they were indistinguishable? Perhaps "yes" and "no" were easy answers; the tough question was, which field to enter? What about the problem of labor in one field taking away from our presence and equally valid labor in another?

Thankfully, no one offered easy, simplistic answers.

Maybe the value was simply in the sharing of questions and frustrations. Or as the man next to me said, "It's just good to be with people whose primary concern isn't how to finance their next BMW."

Would I do it again? Given the chance with that group, I'd go in a minute. I've often thought one way to judge a good movie is how much it echoes into the time after I've seen it. While some films may be pleasurable at the moment, they are quickly forgotten. Others are eminently forgettable. But a few stay with me: an image here, a character there, or a line embedded in the imagination, like a seed that gradually flowers.

It was the same with faith sharing. Our hour together resonated into the week that followed. I remembered especially how one man shared his practice of prayerful pauses. I'd never read about it, never heard it in a lecture, but it made a lot of sense. Asked where he found God, he explained, "I look for the three- to five-minute pauses in my day. Maybe it's walking from my car to my office. Maybe it's a lull between clients, or when I jog. But those short spaces are always there. During them, I think about what's happening in my experience: Is it bringing me closer to the Lord, or drawing me away? Would it help bring another person closer to God?"

"Especially," he continued, "I look at my feelings. Why am I so angry or frustrated? I know if I don't deal with it then, particularly with negative emotions, they can come back to bite me." That reminded me of a wise woman who told the story of the dog scratching at the door. Let the dog in right away, and there's no problem. But ignore it long enough, let the frenzy increase, and the dog's vehemence can tear down the house. So with our uglier emotions, our shadow sides....

In the week after, I set out on a scavenger hunt for prayerful pauses. What was so appealing was their brevity. Few modern-day folks, with multiple commitments and packed schedules, have the chance for the long, uninterrupted, regular stretches of monastic quiet that we traditionally associate with prayer. But three to five minutes was doable!

And those little blips abound. I found a few the first morning: waiting for the car to warm up and the children to emerge for school; waiting for the computer to boot up; waiting for the phone messages to rewind and play; waiting one minute and fifteen seconds (OK, it's on the short side) for coffee to heat in the microwave. Once, those little delays were irritating; after all, I told myself self-righteously, I had work to do, a routine to carry on, people waiting for me! But now I see their beauty: Like a deep draught of oxygen, they put me back in touch with my source, what I am supposed to be all about.

After a while, finding the pauses became a sport: I discovered them at a stoplight, on an elevator, while a cashier made change. My zest for the scavenger hunt made me wonder what I'd done with all that time before I knew about this practice. I suppose I thought of more things to do, where I was going next, what was for dinner, or any one of an infinite number of details that rattle around in the head. Of course they still do—I'm not suggesting that one faith-sharing session changed my mental Muzak to pure Gregorian chant. But it's a start towards a more reflective life, a habit of reading God's text revealed in my experience.

For some time now, I have prayed at the beginning and end of the day; I suspect those are natural markers for many people. I have also come to know the importance of a regularly scheduled day of prayer or retreat for a long, invaluable stretch of simmering. But the brief pause brings the blessings of the longer prayer times into the tiny cracks and almost unnoticeable lulls in the day. For three to five minutes, my day can fill with presence and reflection. No small reward for such a small investment in time....

Like an Earthworm

"But I want to be an earthworm!" my ten-year-old daughter Katie protests plaintively as I lure her from bed on a chilly school morning. I don't pay much attention, my mind on breakfast and the day's schedule. But I take notice later, when she disappears. She needs to eat, dress, load her backpack: Where has she vanished?

I finally find her back in bed, grinning happily. "I'm an earthworm!" she calls with delight, and the description fits: Her brown comforter rolled around her, she snuggles warm as a small creature in the ground. The freckles covering her face provide camouflage as surely as the coloration of a rabbit or mouse.

It looks so appealing, I overcome my guilt and crawl back into bed after I've delivered her to school. Maybe a mom can enjoy being an earthworm, too! The rest of the week, I'll leave home early to give a retreat, get to the office, go to the airport. This morning, I can enjoy the warmth of the blankets and sip an earthenware mug of coffee. Sometimes in prayer, we simply want to be held by God, wordlessly. No Scripture reading, no spiritual books, no formal litany. Just sit with God in gratitude.

The previous night, reading *The Cloister Walk* by Kathleen Norris, I come across a fascinating question. "Who will I be, when loss or crisis or the depredations of time take away the trappings of success, of self-importance, even personality itself?"[1] It strikes with particular poignance now, as I am beginning to amass the trappings, as I struggle to discern how much of my work and commitment is ego-driven, how much is genuine service.

The loss of personality, at this stage in my life, is almost incomprehensible. Then I recall some faces of the elderly in nursing homes: Almost expressionless, reduced to a steady diet of television to fill the time, little change to stimulate, not even the pleasure of a meal to entice, the steady erosion of all that makes life delightful. No one to dress up for; the days are an unchanging sequence of bland robes and shapeless dresses. It's depressing to imagine, and perhaps I worry unnecessarily. Such an old age may not be my fate.

Perhaps I've strayed too far from the earthworm that prompted this prayer-of-sorts. One answer to the question, "who will I be?" might be "the same person I've always been, because the same God creates me." If I lost everything tomorrow, I would burrow into God, held in an embrace that would soothe the losses, drive the tragedies away. Perhaps life would be pared to a bare minimum (whatever an earthworm needs to survive it couldn't be much: dirt? water?), but still God would give me whatever I need.

"What *do* I need?" is a fascinating question. Sometimes God and I disagree on the answer. Sometimes, what seems the absolutely wrong, worst thing is the perfect fulfillment of the need. I remember a day when I'd missed lunch and ran smack up against a case of the 4 P.M. low-blood-sugar blues. What I needed then was nutritionally terrible, but I ate it with zest: a cookie bulging with M&M's in all the gaudiest shades of primary colors. On an ordinary day, I would avoid such a collection of blatantly useless calories. But that day, it was perfect: The resultant burst of energy tided me over till dinner, and I simply wrote off the indulgence as "dessert first."

Sometimes, the people God sends into our lives seem like characters assembled by a neurotic casting director. Just when I need the quiet calm of an introvert, what do I get? You guessed: the noisy brass band of an extrovert. I want someone who'll take care of my needs; I wind up meeting his. The wide variance between what I think I need and what I get suggests that a God with a sense of humor is at play here. As long as we're on the subject of creator and creatures, God must be subtly, mysteriously providing for me just as God does for sparrows—or earthworms?

Since this prayer has rambled far from its wormy starting point, I'll try to tether it back to another early image, a little girl. In another setting, I was sunk deep in prayer at a quiet chapel. That is, until it became impossible to tune out the noises down the corridor as several children ran past.

Then came the small voice saying, "Sorry, Father." She must have been too loud, or interrupted, or tripped outside the aging priest's office.

I cringed inside, waiting for the scolding. Instead, a jovial voice welcomed, "Hannah! How'ya doing?" The elderly priest then gave the little girl a carefully detailed description of his bad knee. How like God our Father, I thought. We go rushing in with the apology or the need we perceive. In an avalanche of welcome, it is totally ignored or turned aside. What matters to God is not the affront. What matters to God is greeting the beloved creature, welcoming the dear child. Even if she is snuggled in bed, pretending to be an earthworm.

Notes

[1] Kathleen Norris, *The Cloister Walk* (New York: Riverhead Books, 1996), p. 295.

You Started It

Sometimes I travel three thousand miles for one good story. Bizarre as it sounds, I often look back over a trip and all I can remember from the blur of airports, people, talks and meals is a single story, the stowaway nugget in my mental luggage. Perhaps that's why when I give a talk, it often becomes a collection of stories, loosely strung together with some theory—the thread that legitimates. I assume my listeners are just like me: After they hang up their clothes and unpack their suitcases, they cling to the one gem—the story.

Anyway, this one came from Henry Mansell, the bishop of Buffalo, New York, a man who impressed me by his knowledge of the Respighi played by the philharmonic orchestra at liturgy. It seems that a man wandered into a welfare office. An intake worker approached him with a stack of forms and began asking the usual questions:

> "Any assets?" she asked, filling in line one.
> "Well, yes: 20,000 shares of IBM, 50,000 of Microsoft, $40,000 in savings," the man replied.
> "What about a home?" she continued.
> "I have three, actually: a cabin in Vail, a house on the coast at Malibu, and an apartment on Lake Shore Drive."
> "Cars?"
> "Yes: a year-old Lexus, and a new BMW."
> Finally, the worker's patience had reached its limit. "This is preposterous!" she exclaimed. "How can you apply for welfare?"
> "Well..." the applicant smiled. "You started it."

We could say the same thing to Jesus, the bishop pointed out. As the ensuing week unfolds, "you started it" becomes a kind of refrain. I look at my children towering over me, two already graduated from college. Could they be those tiny, squalling bundles brought to me in the delivery room? I reflect: "You started small with them, Lord, like mustard seed."

Furthermore, Jesus treated us like rich people: When his

words wafted over the crowd, those who considered themselves scum grew taller with dignity. "Your faith has saved
you," he said repeatedly, emphasizing that the person in
need of healing wasn't merely passive, but brought something to the table. Jesus' encounters weren't one-sided: He
was interested in what people had to say, even his notori-
ously dim apostles. Before he raised Lazarus, who, we pre-
sume, wasn't too articulate at the time, he first held a
lengthy conversation with his sisters.

"You started it" could apply to so many things in our
own lives: the work that has taken on interest and challenge; the acquaintance who has become a dear friend; the
projects which we resisted initially, but which met with unpredictable success; the unpromising house that has become a home; momentum building toward a disaster,
averted at the last minute; or the tragedy that contained the
seeds of treasure.

Each of us could say to God, "Not only did you start it;
you've been there all along, bringing us to where we are
now, a place we would probably not want to trade. The details have fallen into place like the gears of a finely designed
watch or precisely tuned engine."

As I write, I glance up at one of summer's last roses, cut
this morning beneath the gold leaves of October. How long
ago you started it, a seed falling to the ground, a bush grow-
ing for years, transplanted several times and now flowering
in my backyard. The light on its petals gives the shell-pink
tones a special glow. What a long, mysterious sequence of
events brings me to this moment with this flower, or to any
moment, with any person, in any situation. So many factors
could have conspired against our meeting, and yet we are
here. When "here" doesn't look so good, when we're exhausted or doubtful or angry, it's also an opportune time to
remind God, "You got me into this!" It may not have the fi-
nesse of Paul's "and I am confident that you, who began
this good work in us will bring it to completion," but the
thought is similar.

I've often joked with my friends about their feisty

daughters (We're members of a generation more inclined to expect this from our sons. We're so surprised to find this uppityness in our daughters that it merits comment). Inevitably, the facetious refrain sparks the conversation: "Well, where do you think she got it? Couldn't possibly be her *mother*, could it?"

Funny that the cliché "like mother, like daughter" could apply to God. Yet we could easily say, "You treated us like heirs of the Kingdom, cocreators, friends instead of servants. You didn't ask for groveling, but for the joys of our unique gifts. Now we act as if we own the place. What did you expect?" And God, I suspect, smiles with that secret glee of the mother who knows she's been outdone by her child.

You, in your infinite compassion and utmost respect: You started it.

Ocean Depths

The Spiritual Ministry Center in San Diego must be one of the only retreat houses that lists as standard equipment Bibles, bikes and beach towels. The staff is wise enough to take advantage of their greatest asset: the Pacific Ocean crashing on Sunset Cliffs, one block away.

Something in us hungers for that endless expanse of water, as if it symbolized mysteries at once too vast for us to enter and too inviting to resist. The parallels between the sea and spirituality go as far back as the commonplace, "Your sea is so vast and my boat is so small." A sign posted on the coast, "Danger: Unstable Cliffs" seems like a fair warning for those who also approach the hazards of the spiritual life. As Richard Rohr says frequently, human beings are terrified of a love relationship with God. We prefer the safe anesthesia of religion to a relationship that entails so much risk.

But what of those brave enough to risk one tiny toe poked into the foaming surf? What if our inner hunger demands that we follow Christ, knowing that his path leads inexorably to the brutal scene on Calvary? How do we learn more of him, be better friends, seize the courage to be his companions?

The ocean may hold some answers to those questions because like any creation, it speaks clearly of its Creator. Like any good symbol, it contains layers of meaning. To start with the most frothy, we can know the playfulness of God in water spewing over boulders and mist dusting our faces, in spray catching the peachy tones of sunset, sandpipers whose ridiculously skinny legs are perfectly suited to skirting the waves. Best of all, we see God at play in the people on the beach: uninhibited, almost naked, free to run, plunge, skip, twirl, cavort and perform all the zany dance steps they would never risk in the office or the courtroom. With that wondrous rhythm of waves pounding in their ears, they don't seem to care about the sand encroaching into their shorts or the sunburn reddening their backs.

At another level, we see God's faithfulness through the waves rolling relentlessly in. Like sunrise or sunset, they never stop. Visitors leave for a year or two, return, and still find their stately progression. Even people far inland know they're there and take comfort in that reliable presence. So, even when we're exasperated or distraught, we know God is there. Like the ocean we may not see or smell at the moment, God abides. All is well.

Finally, God's care is apparent in the design of the tiniest seashell: the intricacies of its stripes, shades, coloration. For the most minuscule sea creature, God creates a home not only functional but beautiful. The analogy comes quickly: "How much more does God care for you, oh you of little faith?" If God so carefully shelters and adorns marine life, doesn't God also tuck in and take care of me?

In the roar from the seashell, we can almost hear the words, "Didn't I tell you I loved you? Didn't I live it as well as say it? If you couldn't believe my words, could you at least read my life? Trust me in the little things, for starters: a shell, a sand dollar, a drop of salt water. Then we'll build to the bigger picture."

The wave image helps with those transitional times when we hover between worlds, wobbly because we have one foot in each. Crested for a moment before plunging into quieter waters, the coiled arch of a wave is majestic, triumphant. Poised shimmering in the sun, it scintillates with life. So when we are least aware, or even most on edge, we pulse with a mysterious spark. We trust in God's faithfulness; and, now and then, we are lifted, gleaming, into the sun.

Dawn: Grand Canyon

Any experience that leads to awe and wonder comes close to, and can become, prayer. A recent visit to the Grand Canyon confirmed that hunch. I had eagerly anticipated the first sight of the canyon after a sixteen-hour drive, and the sweep of it, the gigantic scale was magnificent. But only after several encounters, when the light played in different ways at different hours of the day, did my appreciation deepen into prayer.

The last time I visited here, I was about ten, the age of the youngest daughter who accompanies me. What a delight to find that the hotels around the rim haven't changed much in all those years: They still have their rustic Forest Service flavor, porch swings, dark wood and big stone fireplaces. In the kiva gift store, we find wonderful treasures: Native American dolls and jewelry that will bring the memory of this journey home. A marker commemorating Stephen Mather, the first director of the National Park System, says simply but profoundly, "There is no end to the good he has done." Wouldn't we all like to be remembered with that epitaph?

At sunset, we sit along the stone walls with tourists from around the world and admire the blue shadows smudging the red rock, the formations highlighted by long fingers of setting sun. Hiking down Bright Angel Trail, each step represents thirty thousand years into the past. History hangs heavily here, with potent reminders of the canyon being carved over the geological ages.

But the canyon on a summer day is inundated by tourists; I want to be alone with it. That urge is strong enough to wake me at 5 A.M. the next morning to watch the sunrise. The phenomenon recurs, of light touching the formations as a symphony conductor would point a baton first to the strings, then to the brass. (I was pleased to discover later that the Grand Canyon has been called "all Beethoven's nine symphonies in stone and magic light.") Because most tourists are not so intrepid (or smitten) and the tourist buses do not roar in at this ungodly hour, a stillness hangs over the canyon, broken only by bird song. I hike the south rim in the solitude enjoyed by the first explorers.

Such a scene, quivering and alive with God's presence and artistry, called forth my highest form of praise. I said a unique form of morning prayer as I raised my arms to the sun and blessed the beauty before me. All the psalms of praise came to mind, as well as a dance for the Native American prayer set to music by David Haas: "Peace before me; peace behind me; peace under my feet." In the luxury of being solitary, I could sing and dance my tribute, with no one to giggle at my lack of singing and dancing ability.

After the trip, I reread "Midnight on the Desert," a favorite essay by J. B. Priestley. About his visit to the Grand Canyon, he wrote, "At last, in all my travels, I had arrived and there had been no anticlimax, and my imagination, after weeks or months of expectant dreaming had not cried, 'Is that all?'"[1]

Cataloguing the beauties, "veils of mist and broken rainbows," "the incredible pageantry of sunlight and chasm," "exquisitely shadowed reddish pinnacles and domes and towers,"[2] Priestley concluded that any efforts to describe the Grand Canyon were useless. He felt that God had set it there in the Arizona desert as a sign, and our words were poor constructs to approach it. But in our wordless appreciation, perhaps we prayed, Priestley and I.

Surely the effects were similar to those of prayer. As he journeyed east to his home in England, and as I drove west from the sunrise, our response was the same. "I felt wonder and awe, but at the heart of them a deep rich happiness. I had seen [God's] handiwork, and I rejoiced."[3]

Notes

[1] J. B. Priestley, *Midnight on the Desert* (New York: Harper, 1939), p. 283.
[2] Priestley, p. 284.
[3] Priestley, p. 288.

Part Five

※

Seasonal Prayer

Changes in the seasons can lift the heart. The soft hush of the first snowfall, the surprise of violets in February, the fragrance of lilacs, rain falling on newly cut grass, a harvest moon, pine scent in December: The sensate image wakens a deeper self, who prays with the rich rhythms of nature.

Prayer has a different coloration in April than it does in November. This wisdom is reflected in the Church's liturgical cycle. The word *Lent* means "spring"; the parallels between Easter and nature's green resurrection have often been drawn. Pentecostal fire warms us as winter's chill has finally faded. Advent's still waiting occurs in the darkest season of the year; the light of Christmas breaks when the days begin to lengthen again.

The incarnation of Christ blessed all embodied creatures, whose senses respond alertly to the seasons. Celebrating the diversity of seasons and the gift of the body, we turn to seasonal prayer...

New Year's Reflections

Sometimes our inadequacies become a woeful litany: the crabby note dashed off to a friend; the promised snack forgotten, leaving the fifth grade desolate and hungry; the college financial aid application lost in the swirl of other forms due the same day. That litany of trivia doesn't begin to touch the dark currents within, the far worse sins that insult the coworker, ignore the hurting and damage the beloved.

Without dragging out the condemnations any further, those of us who spend this time of year in serious stock-taking become quickly convinced of our enormous human limitations: whether in working or in parenting or in ordering our loves. It's tempting to turn to God in despair and say, "How can I ever cope with all you have given me? Don't you know how powerless I am?"

How would God answer? Trying to take God's viewpoint, I thought: What if I had a child who was physically challenged in hearing or vision, but who still tried desperately to keep up, to please? Wouldn't I have an aching empathy for that child? It's not an enormous leap to extrapolate from that feeling to God's empathy for God's blundering children. "If you, then, who are evil, know how to give good gifts to your children, how much more will your Father in heaven give good things to those who ask him!" (Matthew 7:11).

Through the metaphor of parenting, we can glimpse the way God must regard our efforts—knowing that we lack so much, but we try so hard. God must see that struggle with such profound compassion that it takes on flesh and becomes a person, Jesus, to go with us.

God speaks in Isaiah 43:3-4: "I give Egypt as your ransom,... [b]ecause you are precious in my sight,/ and honored, and I love you,/ I give people in return for you,/ nations in exchange for your life." Today that might translate to, "I give Hawaii for you, or France, or Japan, or a whole nation's beauty and wealth." Even better, it becomes, "I give my son for you."

We miss the full power of that gift because we hear it too often; we take it for granted. I was jolted into a glimmer of understanding recently, when I saw a film about a blind man running a marathon with a sighted companion, who steered him, held his arm on steps, guided him around obstacles, called out warnings and support.

A similar dynamic occurs regularly on the ski slopes of Colorado, where a blind skier wearing a distinctive vest is accompanied by a sighted skier who provides verbal cues and encouragement. Often the companion is college-aged, intent on the task, peering ahead to anticipate problems, trying to see doubly hard, as if for two. The main reason I ski is the scenery: seeing the froth of snow-crested peaks piling like waves against the sky. For the blind skier, something must compensate for missing that dimension. I suspect it may be the guide, a young person so lavish with praise and generous with encouragement that blind skiers flock to the slopes.

At times we all find ourselves in the role of blind runner or skier. We become caught in dilemmas where we simply say, "I can't handle this. I don't know what to do. Help me out." It's hardly the most eloquent of prayers, but maybe the most meaningful. Through that prayer, we turn to God as to our sighted companion.

God's response may be so subtle we do not even recognize it. It might take the form of a friend's casual comment that is precisely what we needed to hear when we needed to hear it. It could be the gift of unanticipated time, money or sympathy. It might come as sleep when we are exhausted or stimulation when we are bored. God's language is varied and complex, but the signals penetrate the darkness as surely as the cues given by the guide. God is inclined toward us, bending over us, breathing into us just as on the first day of creation. That tender concern never stops; if anything, it grows more intense when we wander in darkness.

Consequently, we make the worst mistakes when we try to assume the burden of doing it all, and doing it alone.

No wonder we crash in exhaustion, cynicism or apathy. We miss all the whispered messages assuring us that we're not alone, and forget our faithful companion.

An eloquent reminder comes through the promise God makes in Isaiah: "When you pass through the waters, I will be with you,/ and through the rivers, they shall not overwhelm you;/ when you walk through fire you shall not be burned,/ and the flame shall not consume you" (43:2).

If prayer is a dialogue, then Archbishop Oscar Romero seems to have phrased the realistic human response to that confident promise. He writes,

> We cannot do everything,
> and there is a sense of liberation in realizing that. This
>   enables us to do something, and to do it very well.
> It may be incomplete,
> but it is a beginning,
> a step along the way,
> an opportunity for the Lord's grace to enter and do the
>   rest.[1]

In many ways we have limited vision. We cannot see far enough, deep enough, broad enough. Yet we know instinctively where to turn for help. The promise of the coming year encourages us, despite our past failings, to "do something." Maybe Romero's prayer—and ours—is the blind hand groping for the faithful guide in the dark.

Notes

[1] Quoted in James Dunning, *Echoing God's Word* (Arlington, Va.: The North American Forum on the Catechumenate, 1993), p. 380.

Learning to Follow: Palm Sunday

That Palm Sunday, the reading of the Passion lay over us like a veil. We couldn't see it clearly or brush it aside, but we knew its certain presence there. If we were truly followers of this crucified Lord, what else could more surely shape and define our parish community?

According to that reading, we follow a failure—one who had tenderly fed his friends, spoken with poignant beauty at their final meal and tried to heal the violence of thugs with swords—but who nonetheless hung stripped, tortured, his life drained, his mission unfinished. The friends he'd trusted abandoned him; in a stinging question, he wondered if even God had forsaken him.

How ironic: we hear this story dressed-for-success, primed to tackle our various spheres tomorrow and *accomplish*. We'll arrange details efficiently, complete projects, finalize deals. We'll go home from school or office tomorrow evening proud of ourselves. We've tied up the loose ends— yes, siree—left no stone unturned, achieved justice and right the American way! (Trumpets, please.)

Does the silence from Calvary mock us? Or does the symbol find expression in other ways, in the places we'd least suspect? Is Christ more truly present in our failures and sadnesses, the loneliness at twilight, the head sunk in the hands? The welts on his back and the scars on his cheeks: do they surface in our insurmountable problems, our unredeemed failures? Is he there in the exhaustion and doubt as well as the celebration? Is he as present to us when we betray as when we anoint? Wanting to be Mary with her ointment, we all know that at times, we're Judas with his lousy silver. Perhaps the innocent suffer the most complete identification. A paranoid schizophrenic once told me, "We who are mentally ill wear the crown of thorns all the time."

"We would see Jesus," said the disciples, and we echo their yearning. Maybe we're puzzled because we look in the wrong places. We want answers and solutions, when all that beckons is the way of the cross. All we want, we say, is someone to tell us how to live and how to get it right and how to remain serene in the face of chaos and how to fix everything that's wrong. "Meanwhile," in the words of Thomas Merton, "Christ is in agony until the end of time."

If there is an answer to this irony, a way to appreciate this paradox, the liturgy gives us the clue. We are told to pick up our crosses and follow. So, with varying degrees of understanding, we begin Holy Week in procession, accompanying each other. Our action becomes a response to the questions raised by Maryknoll Sister Ita Ford before her martyrdom in El Salvador:

> Can I say to my neighbors, "I have no solutions to the situation, I don't know the answers, but I will walk with you, be with you?" Can I let myself be evangelized by this opportunity?[1]

Sometimes it is easier to appreciate the cross in another's life than in our own. I can recognize the agony of the recently widowed, the parents whose child has not improved after a series of surgeries, or the neighbor who has lost his job. But can I identify my own cross?

Can we see our struggles with priorities, our difficulties with relationships, our financial crises, our stresses and constant deprivation of time and energy in light of Calvary? Maybe so, maybe not. But we press on. The words of Elizabeth Ann Seton, "we make the path by walking," have become almost a cliché. But they are especially true in the context of Christ's passion. We don't get quick fixes; we find a path. We learn to follow by following.

Notes

[1] Megan McKenna, *Lent: The Daily Readings* (Maryknoll, N.Y.: Orbis Books, 1997), p. 175.

Mother's Day

I have spent the week in dialogue with a most unusual woman. In hands which should cradle a child, she holds a crown of thorns. Her fingers are seared as brutally as her son or daughter's flesh was torn. She is the Mother of the Disappeared. While this icon might seem an odd choice for the celebration of Mother's Day, it is appropriate for reasons larger than Hallmark cards and florist's bouquets. Her halo reminds us that the parents of the martyred die inwardly like Mary and are holy like Mary.

Violating all the rules for classic iconography, a handprint smears the lower left corner of her portrait. It is as out of place as a jelly blob on a book, a stain on the new carpet, or the grubby marks that children leave on walls. Lest we become too heady about holiness, it reminds us of reality. Meeting this icon, I protested, "I don't want to live with you all week! Your stare condemns my safety and luxury. Why don't you go away and let me enjoy the apple blossoms, my daughter's pastel dresses, the joys of spring?" My instinct to flee seemed supported by a line from the gospel: "I came that they might have life in abundance." If Christ's gift of life has been so cruelly grabbed from these mothers and their children, what does it mean to me?

She replies, "I participate in Christ's trouncing of the death-dealing forces that stalk all children. Just as the martyrs of El Salvador played their part in bringing an end to the civil war, so I stand implacable as conscience. Persistently, I call oppressors to accountability. Furthermore, I challenge you to nurture the life you have been given, for it is fragile and precious."

Her eyes upon me quiet my annoyance with my children, my frustration with their little failures. She reminds me that although I may not undergo her particular ordeal, I may confront other problems. Can I bring to them her serenity, her conviction that God is with us both in loving support?

"You still have your children," she reminds me.

"Cherish them. Why do you get irritated when they invade your quiet times? I would give anything for such a little invasion. But my arms are empty. My home is silent."

Her ache is not unique to Third World mothers. After Jean Donovan was martyred in El Salvador, her mother Pat wrote:

> For nine months I carried you under my heart.
> Now you live in my heart forever.
> Sometimes I forget—
> I see a blouse you'd like or a pair of jeans.
> I feel a fist in my stomach—
> There's no one to buy them for![1]

Because I have not experienced the tragedy these mothers have, I feel pampered by comparison. Yet Madeleine L'Engle cautions, "the icon becomes idol when any one part of the body wants the rest of the body to be just like it.... How odd it would be if the body were all hands or knees or teeth!" Something terrible in the icon's gaze forgives my security and calls me to that shared sanctity which transcends our differences.

Eventually, for me as for her, all the children disappear. They grow up, leave for college, find their own paths. As one mom lamented, sweeping up debris, "First they break your things. Then they break your heart." Sometimes the mothers disappear. My ten-year-old daughter tells me about the little boy in her class who made a Mother's Day card along with the other children, but he didn't know where to send it. Mom left; he lives with dad.

In such heartbreaking separation, we see into the mystery of God. God says of the beloved people Israel: "How can I give you up?... My heart recoils within me;/ my compassion grows warm and tender" (Hosea 11:8). Jesus, torn from his mother on the way to Calvary, can understand our worst nightmare, and relate to the suffering we most dread. However difficult our experience with our children may be, God participates intimately in the relationship. And that is good news for Mother's Day.

Notes

[1] Quoted in Rosemary Radford Ruether, *Women-Church* (San Francisco: Harper & Row, 1985), p. 233.

Gone Fishin'

It's a family ritual. Every July or August we fill up the station wagon with enough boxes to make it sag, wedge in kids and fishing poles, and head for the hills.

Our vacation at Pearl Lake is an annual escape from city heat, depressing headlines and job stress. For five days we live beside a mountain lake. We breathe air scented with clover and eat freshly caught trout. We hike, row boats, trap crawdads, and recount every corny story we have accumulated during twelve years of coming here.

Our time together eludes any lampoon on the family vacation. Over the years it has become a ritual. On the ride up, crankiness may sizzle and irritability may spread like a sticky stain on the car upholstery. But recognizing familiar landmarks changes the mood. We spot the river, the general store, finally the cabin.

Our activities have become family traditions. The Hot Dog Roast, Popcorn and Pictionary. Hiking through the Mount Zirkel Wilderness. The Safari to the General Store for Ice Cream. Rowing to the Dam. Fly Fishing on the Yampa River. No one follows a schedule, but everyone knows that if we don't include these events we'll leave feeling cheated.

Even as I relish this special time, I know that vacations are a luxury many families cannot afford, that our proximity to the Rocky Mountains and access to this log cabin are rare blessings, and that the stresses many families endure would make a time such as this unthinkable.

But I also know what it does for our health as individuals and for our sense of belonging to each other. I have read about the value of ritual and of time deliberately spent just *being* rather than doing. So I do not apologize when I leave my colleagues gnashing their teeth over deadlines. Their turns will come, too, and I will cover for them, convinced that everyone should have a week in July or August and a place like Pearl. Here I learn firsthand why Thomas Merton said, "It is essential to experience all the times and moods of one good place."

Sometimes in January or February, falling asleep after a day spent battling snow, I mentally retrace my daily walk around the lake. The colors are brilliant: white trunks of aspen against evergreen, all mirrored in the water's pewter surface. The wildflowers bend with the long grass: purple and yellow daisies, blue lupine, Queen Anne's lace, Indian paintbrush. Hummingbirds flash past; the sandhill crane warbles its haunting cry. Beauty surprises at every turn: here a chiseled mountain face, there a trail lined with the white candles of flowers. As Dostoevsky wrote, "One good memory may be the means of saving us."

Other people use New Year's Eve as a marker for time. For me, the day we arrive triggers memories of the year that has passed since we came here last. Like any other year, it has had its high points: my daughter's college scholarship, my award for poetry, meetings with inspiring people, a day of perfect spring skiing, a bottle of white zinfandel shared with close friends. It has also had its low points: tragic news of deaths and illnesses, disagreements with teenagers, accidents, rejections, financial woes.

But even as I experienced all that, the lake lay placidly, in season and out, its shores brittle with frost as well as tapestried with wildflowers. Clouds of all weathers had been reflected in its surface; the forest had gone through its whole cycle: fiery golds to bare branches to the full leafy greens shading the path in patches.

The lake is a metaphor for something more transcendent than a body of water. How like the love of God it is. We wax warm and cold; we rage and praise; we wander oblivious—and occasionally we remember. God remains constant: all fullness, all nurture, all kindness. We move within that Holy One like fish in water or birds in air, often unaware, yet always sustained and supported.

The mystics referred to the inexhaustibility of God's depths as *iepectasis*. John wrote, "from his fullness we have all received" (John 1:16). Some may taste it in contemplation, music, service or relationships, but I find it here in a deep blue lake sequined by sun. Like William Butler Yeats,

> I hear lake water lapping with low sounds by the shore;
> While I stand on the roadway, or on the pavements grey
> I hear it in the deep heart's core.[1]

What does this have to do with prayer? Maybe nothing.
Maybe everything.

Notes

[1] William Butler Yeats, "The Lake Isle of Innisfree" in *Selected Poems and Two Plays of William Butler Yeats* (New York: Macmillan, 1962), p. 13.

Under a Golden Tree

What could prompt October prayer better than this tree? The air is crisp, newly washed with last night's rain. One tree in the backyard has turned early, against the darker background of trees still green. Didn't artists weave ancient tapestries like this, one gold thread precious against more muted colors?

So I sit, with my coffee and my tree, and relish this time of transition. Every other Friday morning in the month ahead, I'll be running through an airport, catching a flight. Perhaps it is the edge of that travel pressing close that helps me sink into the serenity, appreciating this lull. When that time comes, I will probably enjoy the bubble of voices, the stimulation of new stories, flavors and sounds, but for now I savor the lull: home.

It's humbling for one who makes her living crafting words to realize that she could not add a syllable to the grandeur of the tree before me. How arrogant it would be to attempt it—and perhaps it's even arrogant to try to capture those colors on paper now. It stands as perfect prayer, giving praise and glory to God. Looking up through the canopy, I find a new image for joy: golden feathers brushing a cobalt sky. What more can the tiny human at the tree's foot do, other than add her gratitude?

As the light strikes different clusters of leaves, the shades turn: here a darker mustard, there a buttery yellow. I ask that blessings might pour on those I love like the rain of light cascading onto branches. Our family is fairly settled now into our fall routine, the children comfortable in school. The switch from an easier summer schedule is no longer sharply defined; we have grown as accustomed to the autumn rhythm as we have to warmer clothes. The increased commitments seem as natural as jeans and sweatshirts, our shorts and sandals stashed for next summer.

Usually I fight the end of summer, dreading the rigidity of school schedules, the burden of homework and early alarm clocks. For three months, I like the children all home:

the noise, the laughter and energy spill into the yard; the flowers flourish. At first, the quiet, empty house after Labor Day seems as formal and unnatural as tight shoes or a scratchy shirt. Now, however, back-to-school has become a second skin, and we are enjoying the season's fruits.

Maybe it all ties in with harvest: bringing work to completion after the gestation of lazy summer days. Much as I love having the family home, I'll concede that the increase in laundry and cooking drains time, and it's harder to write with constant interruptions. Even now, in relative calm, there's too much work and sometimes it's tedious. But then I ask myself, would I rather go back to a time when the children were infants, no school beckoned and I was a full-time mom? That was work of a different kind, to which I would not return happily. No, I enjoy the colleagues, the challenges and the rewards of this stage in life, suspecting with many of my middle-aged friends that youth is overrated.

Now if only we in the harvest of our lives could glow with the life of this tree. Usually I dislike art that's gilded or clothes that are sequined. Yet God's creation is brash as trombone here, scintillating like copper, resounding like a brass quintet. Perhaps through it God says, "Now that I've got your attention...."

In her book *Dear Heart, Come Home*, Joyce Rupp describes an understanding that came in her late forties. While she had grown up on a farm, she learned later in life that the strong sense of God's presence she felt while with the earth was secondary to the kinds of prayer learned in more formal religious education.

> My religion, and the voice of spiritual authorities within it, seemed to say that my prayer and major spiritual impetus should especially be with the Scriptures, with the Eucharist, and with my relationships. While I did have a sense of God and an occasional revelation of the inner journey in those places, none was ever comparable to the immanent, intense, mystical experiences I had when I spent contemplative time with the earth.[1]

"Anytime I was with the earth in a contemplative mode, I

found a taste of honey for my soul,"[2] she continues. Yet, warned about the heresy of pantheism, she dismissed the pull to nature as a less important connection with God.

In the harvest of mid-life, Rupp finally realized that nature "was the primary way I was meant to 'find' the divine presence."[3] Her readers and admirers, vicariously observing her discovery unfold, might cheer with the brazen orange tones of this tree. "Yes!" we want to shout rowdily. Prayer isn't always hushed, pious, contained in the walls of church. It doesn't require bowed heads, books and vestments. Sometimes it comes spontaneously as a shout in the Psalms, the bear hug of a grand reunion, the glorious timpani of trees.

Notes

[1] Joyce Rupp, *Dear Heart, Come Home* (New York: Crossroad Publishing Co., 1996), p. 125.
[2] Rupp, p. 92.
[3] Rupp, p. 93.

November Prayer

One November, my spiritual director suggested his own prayer practice: each day, being grateful for one person, one event, one material blessing and one spiritual blessing in his life. It tied into an earlier discussion we'd had, on how an "attitude of gratitude" could offset much of the despair, discourtesy and general whininess that seemed to characterize our era. It seemed appropriate that our family celebration of Thanksgiving not be simply an isolated event, but a crescendo, a climax of thanks strung throughout the month.

As it turned out, thirty-one days weren't enough for all the praise. Choosing one person each day was the hardest. Images of my immediate family rushed in at once, but I put them on hold to reach for people I thought of less often. I remembered the first English teacher who recognized and encouraged my writing ability, when I was a nerdy high-school sophomore. Now she's eighty years old and blind, living in a retirement home and listening to my books on tape. I included friends I'd lost contact with over time, who were there at crucial moments, as well as friends and colleagues who bless each day with their humor and reliability. Total strangers who'd welcomed me into their communities for an intense day of workshops or prayer, relatives, mentors, doctors: as the month went on, I began to recognize a whole community of saints who at various times had been Christ's face or voice or touch to me.

My list of events contained the high drama of a wedding, birth, award or graduation as well as the simple loveliness of a picnic by the lake or a hike in the forest. The event could be as quick as good news on the phone or as sustained as a restful vacation. Yesterday's sunset, an unexpected compliment, a check in the mail, a good meal: they all made the roster of events to be met with gratitude.

Material blessings ranged from clean sheets to a vanilla latte. A comfortable dress, a stimulating book, a good movie, jet travel, efficient phones, computers and highway systems—in this country, we pay attention to such comforts only when we lack them or they break down. In other countries, the miracle comes when the electricity is on or the phone works. As the weather chills each November and many families face homelessness, I'm grateful for the little click in the night that means the furnace is turning on. While all the categories overlapped, I found it hardest to distinguish which blessings were explicitly spiritual. But I included an uplifting liturgy with music I hummed all week and a homily that resonated days after I heard it. Gratitude filled me for a time of restorative prayer after a week of exhausting detail.

While others might not agree, I placed poetry, sunsets and a deep conversation with a dear friend in the "spiritual blessings" list.

The beauty of this kind of prayer is that it's so uniquely personal. It helped me see how directly and intimately God calls my name and reaches me. Even if I had an identical twin, her list would be different. Even the people closest to me would probably not thank God for the same things. And if I heard another's prayer, I might be startled: Why didn't I think of that?

The previous November had been a difficult month. I remember it clearly because a good friend died, disagreement ripped apart a close group of my coworkers and the weather seemed unusually harsh. Depression shadowed the month, dark as wet mahogany leaves crushed underfoot. It seemed like spring—or even Advent—would never come.

But this November was different. I'll admit the weather was better—a string of warm, golden days that eased the transition to winter. Nothing particularly traumatic occurred. But I suspect the primary difference has been internal. "The color of one's thought dyes one's soul"—and in turn one's experience, said Marcus Aurelius. If our prayer wells with gratitude, how can praise not spill into our days? If we focus on all we've been given, how can we fret ungratefully over what we lack?

Christmas Memories

The fragrances of Christmas trigger memories. The morning after we put up our tree the house is filled with the scent of fresh pine. We breakfast in the soft glow of the tree's lights, and I remember a Christmas in July...

July Fourth, to be exact. Having planned the usual summer festivities, my husband and I brought nine teenagers and an eight-year-old to a mountain condo to celebrate. Then the blizzard hit. "Crazy Colorado weather!" tourists chuckled, and wondered whether they could glimpse the evening fireworks through the grey clouds. Sulkily scrapping plans for barbecues and volleyball beneath the peaks, our troupe plodded through the wet forest to the indoor swimming pool.

And sitting beside the pool, I grew inordinately thankful for the whole nutty mess. The kids had adapted to the moody weather and were happily cavorting in the water, perfecting their seal imitations. So much life surged in them, and I thought of the source: "I came that they may have life, and have it abundantly" (John 10:10).

Unplanned and unpredictable as mountain weather, Incarnation blessed the swimming pool that day, and I thanked a God who took on human skin. He hadn't just camped out for a while until things got tough. As Nancy Mairs writes in *Ordinary Time*, "He was human, remember. When you're human, you're human all the way. No calling a halt to the condition when things get nasty, saying: 'Enough for me. I'll be off now.'"[1]

A certain steel underlies the sweetness of the manger scene—the hay, the infant, the angel song—because the God who came in innocence would stay through the brutality. Even the beginning of Jesus' life seemed to prove he would endure the whole mixed bag. Balancing the terrible inconvenience of travel late in pregnancy, the cool ostracism of the innkeeper and the dirt of the stable were the starlight, the warm shelter, the kindness of shepherds, the joy of the Magi, the safety of Egypt.

God came in something small, like a baby: something humble, like swaddling; something unnoticed, like a stable. Jesus coming as an infant recalls the power of the power-less, the tower of the tiny. His advent made every ordinary house a dwelling for holiness. So we festoon the fireplace, hang holly from the chandelier, place vanilla candles on the window sills and tuck sprigs of evergreen in every nook and bookcase. Aromatic reminders that where we are, God is. Our turf, however cluttered, is holy ground.

Perhaps this year I am more appreciative of cookies baking, bread rising and carols playing. Such a sensual feast contrasts with last Christmas, when all I smelled was hospital antiseptic and my only ritual was changing bloody dressings. Our oldest son, home on holiday, was attacked at a football game, and had surgery two days before Christmas. The whole ordeal brought home the fact that our society is becoming increasingly violent.

But violence played a part in that first Christmas, too. Herod breathed vengeance on the innocent when his paranoid control was threatened. We frost the manger scene in sugary icing, but the original version must have held traces of fear and confusion. "No room in the inn" sounds quaint—unless you're in labor. The cattle low sweetly—until you imagine the stink.

Last Christmas made me more realistic and helped me see how intimately I participate in this message of incarnation. As I leaned over chrome bed rails toward my anesthetized son, I knew the same emotion that drives the whole feast: a mother's love for her child. I had come to Christmas by a different path: not the usual shopping malls and parties, but the kindness of teenagers who waited in the recovery room, the slow stages of healing, the empathy of friends.

I met a God who didn't use glory to win human reverence. My drowsy, bandaged son in his most vulnerable moments evoked the deepest affection, like God as a human infant. Walter Wink writes, "We simply do not know the limits of the redeeming power of the small. Perhaps there are none." Funny, when my son skis black diamond runs, no one applauds. But when he sat up for the first time after the operation and took a sip of water, I was ecstatic. Last Christmas attuned me to small joys and little treasures.

Jesus chose to live in the ordinary context of a human family like ours. His choice forever blessed our clumsy efforts to gift each other and to make our home beautiful. Hasidic wisdom says everyone should have two pockets. In one a slip of paper reads, "I am only dust and ashes." In the other, a paper proclaims, "For me alone the entire universe has been created." For me, God became human.

We celebrate the second message today. Light the candles. Hang the wreaths. Inhale clear, cold air and the aroma of evergreen. Bring on the smells of Christmas that lead into the evocative terrain of memory.

Notes

[1] Nancy Mairs, *Ordinary Time: Cycles in Marriage, Faith and Renewal* (Boston: Beacon Press, 1993).

BIBLIOGRAPHY

Barry, William A. *Paying Attention To God: Discernment in Prayer.* Notre Dame, Ind.: Ave Maria Press, 1990.

Beckett, Wendy. *The Gaze of Love.* San Francisco: HarperSanFrancisco, 1994.

_____. *Meditations on Joy.* New York: DK Publishing, Inc., 1995.

Brown, Robert McAfee. *Observer in Rome: A Protestant Report on the Vatican Council.* Garden City, N.Y.: Doubleday, 1964.

Coffey, Kathy. "Prayer and Action, Action and Prayer: An Interview with Mary Luke Tobin," *Praying* 35 (March/April, 1990).

De Waal, Esther. *A Seven Day Journey With Thomas Merton.* Ann Arbor, Mich.: Servant Publications, 1992.

Donnelly, Doris. *Spiritual Fitness.* New York: HarperSanFrancisco, 1993.

Dunning, James. *Echoing God's Word.* Arlington, Va.: The North American Forum on the Catechumenate, 1993.

Eliot, T.S. "Four Quartets," *Collected Poems.* San Diego: Harcourt, Brace and World, 1963.

Frost, Robert. "Birches," in *Literature: the Human Experience,* ed. Richard Abcarian and Marvin Klotz. New York: St. Martin's Press, 1984.

Futrell, John C. and Marian Cowan. *The Spiritual Exercises of Saint Ignatius of Loyola: A Handbook for Directors.* Hartford, Conn.: Jesuit Educational Center for Human Development, Inc., 1988.

Johnson, Elizabeth. *She Who Is: The Mystery of God in Feminist Theological Discourse.* New York: Crossroad Publishing Co., 1992.

Karris, Robert J. *Luke: Artist and Theologian: Luke's Passion Account as Literature*. New York: Paulist Press, 1985.

Kavanaugh, John. *The Word Encountered: Meditations on the Sunday Scriptures*. Maryknoll, N.Y.: Orbis Books, 1996.

Lynch, William. "Death as Nothingness," *Continuum 5* (Fall, 1967), pp. 459-469.

Mairs, Nancy. *Ordinary Time: Cycles in Marriage, Faith and Renewal*. Boston: Beacon Press, 1993.

McEnroy, Carmel. *Guests in Their Own House: The Women of Vatican II*. New York: Crossroad, 1996.

McKenna, Megan. *Lent: The Daily Readings*. Maryknoll, N.Y.: Orbis Books, 1997.

Mitchell, Nathan. *Eucharist as Sacrament of Initiation*. Chicago: Liturgy Training Publications, 1994.

Moynahan, Michael. *Orphaned Wisdom: Meditations for Lent*. Mahwah, N.J.: Paulist Press, 1990.

Norris, Kathleen. *The Cloister Walk*. New York: Riverhead Books, 1996.

Nouwen, Henri J. *Can You Drink the Cup?* Notre Dame, Ind.: Ave Maria Press, 1996.

Oliver, Mary. "The Summer Day," *New and Selected Poems*. Boston: Beacon Press, 1992.

Priestley, J. B. *Midnight on the Desert*. New York: Harper, 1939.

Ruether, Rosemary Radford. *Women-Church*. San Francisco: Harper & Row, 1985.

Riso, Don Richard. *Enneagram Transformations*. Boston: Houghton Mifflin, 1993.

Rupp, Joyce. *Dear Heart, Come Home*. New York: Crossroad Publishing Co., 1996.

Sobrino, Jon. *Companions of Jesus*. Maryknoll, N.Y.: Orbis Books, 1990.

Toolan, David. "Some Biographical Reflections on William F. Lynch's Thought," in *American Catholic Traditions: Resources for Renewal*, ed. Sandra Yocum Mize and William Portier. Annual Publication of the College Theology Society, Vol. 42. Maryknoll, N.Y.: Orbis Books, 1997.

Tyler, Anne. *Dinner at the Homesick Restaurant*. New York: Knopf, 1982.

Vanauken, Sheldon. *A Severe Mercy*. San Francisco: Harper & Row, 1977.

Yeats, William Butler, "The Lake Isle of Innisfree" in *Selected Poems and Two Plays of William Butler Yeats*. New York: Macmillan, 1962.

PERMISSIONS